Making the Wilderness Your Home

Making the Wilderness Your Home

An illustrated guide to living in the woods.

James E. Churchill

ICS Books, Inc.
Merrillville, Indiana

Making the Wilderness Your Home

Printed in U.S.A.

Published by:
ICS BOOKS, Inc.
1000 E. 80th Place
Merrillville, IN 46410

Library of Congress Cataloging-in-Publication Data

Churchill, James E., 1934-
  Making the wilderness your home.

  Includes index.
  1. Home economics, Rural — United States. 2. Home economics, Rural—Canada. 3. Outdoor life—United States. 4. Outdoor life—Canada. 5. Wilderness survival—United States. 6. Wilderness survival—Canada. I. Title.
TX23.C47 1987   640   87-4134
ISBN 0-934802-33-5

Table of Contents

Chapter 1.
Can You Take
To The Wilderness

Most Americans are descended from hardy pioneer stock. Our ancestors left Europe with only the clothes on their backs because they felt the very human need to have the freedom to accomplish whatever they were capable of. It required courage and fortitude to leave the mother country for an uncertain future, and it tended to weed out the timid and slothful.

Because they were superior people, the hardy immigrants who did reach the shores of America succeeded in establishing the mightiest nation that has ever risen on this earth. But, something happened as we attained riches and security. We fouled our air, polluted our water and erected concrete and steel jungles that are called cities.

We have also produced legions of people who feel an unfull-filled ache in their hearts. They would gladly trade life in the urban environment for a chance to be their own person on their own land, where the water is clear, the air is scented with pines, and wildlife can be seen from their windows. Call it wilderness or call it woods, many believe this is the place to find the finest kind of life.

1

If you are one of these people, this book is written for you. Regardless of your age, your background or your income, if you want to live your life in your own way, this book can set you free.

I say this because my family and I did it and we have no special qualifications. We have lived for 11 deeply enjoyable and satisfying years where our neighbor is nearly one mile away and deer greatly outnumber the human population. We can walk out the back door and if we kept to a certain route, walk for days without encountering a town or even a dwelling. The following reprint of a magazine story that appeared in *Outdoor Life* magazine gives an account of how we made our way.

My family and I live in the woods in northern Wisconsin. We do exactly as we please, which means that I spend most of my time hunting and fishing. Our children are healthy and happy and doing well. My wife has all the appliances and other labor-saving aids that she wants to ease her housework. Almost all of the people we know are happy and relaxed. Our income is adequate, and if we needed more money we could acquire it without sacrificing much. We have given up no advantages and have gained a new life. I believe that anyone can do the same if they are tough and self-reliant, but here is the way we went about forging the good life.

I nagged at my wife, Joan, until she said, "OK, Jim, I'll move when we have a place to move to."

Soon afterward I started moonlighting at a variety of part-time jobs. I also quit smoking and cut out all recreation and every luxury that I was addicted to. In four years, we have saved enough money to buy 40 acres of land in the least populated county in northern Wisconsin. There was a decrepit hunting cabin on it.

The first year after we bought the place only my son and I went to the cabin with any regularity. Gradually my wife and daughter started coming along. Finally we were spending all of our vacations in the north woods. Each time we went, the quiet, wooded setting with its clear air, deep blue lakes and unspoiled forests claimed a little more of us.

One Sunday afternoon 11 years ago, we were going home from the cabin and got caught in the usual 100-mile traffic jam of vacationers returning to the Milwaukee area. We saw a helicopter land on the other side of the highway to pick up some bloody, mangled victims of a traffic accident. After the helicopter disappeared, I said to Joan, "Here we are, risking our lives and the lives of our kids almost every weekend to spend a few precious hours in the north woods. Don't you think it's time to move up there permanently?"

To my everlasting wonder she nodded her head yes.

The next morning we listed our house with a real-estate agent, and soon we had a buyer. I gave notice at work, and we worked feverishly to get things ready for the move. Finally the big day came, and we loaded our possessions into our pickup and two rented trailers and started north. Jim Jr., who has been called Trapper since he was very young, drove a sedan pulling one trailer. With him were our beagle Pokie, my daughter Jolain and her dog Missy. Joan and I led the way with the pickup and the other trailer.

We drove the 300 miles to Florence County turned off Route 70 and followed the Edith Lake Firelane to our drive.

"That's a road?" Jolain asked. "It looks more like a hay field."

Indeed it did. I had to walk ahead so we could see where to drive through the four-foot grass. We finally arrive at the ramshackle hunting cabin and unloaded. The next day Trapper and I said goodbye to the ladies and drove back to our former home to get a tractor that we had bought to use in our new life.

We got back to the house at 2 P.M., started the tractor and pointed north. While one of us drove the tractor, the other followed in the pickup. We had more than 300 miles to travel since we had to stay on winding secondary roads because of the low speed of the tractor. Twenty-five hours later we finally drove the tractor down the grass choked lane to our new home.

The next morning Trapper and I started selecting a site for our new cabin while Joan and Jolain busied themselves at sprucing up the hunting cabin. I believe on that day our family became closer than ever would have been possible otherwise as we all started working together to make a success of our new life.

We found a building site on a welldrainded slope close to our old cabin. Our first step was to clear the site with a chain saw, axe, shovel, pick and tractor. It was grueling work. It was already the first of September and we didn't want to live in the old cabin during the harsh winter.

We had decided to build and A-frame. We liked the treelike lines of its long sloping roof because it would shed snow, and we decided the simple design wouldn't require skilled carpentry work. We could do all the work ourselves. It also seemed to be the most economical type of structure to build.

The first step was to dig holes for the footings that would support the building. Then we dug sand from a nearby hillside, mixed it with cement and water to form concrete, and poured the concrete into the holes. When it dried, we had two rows of sturdy pillars. The house frame would stand on these pillars. Every morning we'd get up at 4:30 or 5:00 A.M. and work until dark. When Joan wasn't cooking meals for us, she helped in any way she could. In two weeks the frame was done. Then we nailed a plywood covering over it. The next step was to put shingles on the roof. Once disaster nearly struck.

Joan and I were standing on a board near the top of the building, tacking on long rows of shingles, when suddenly our support broke. "We're falling!" she screamed. We fell more than 20 feet to the ground. Miraculously neither of us was hurt, except for scrapes on our knees and forearms. Joan took the rest of the day off, and I went back to work, but my hands shook for a while. Finally we were ready to have the electrical wiring put in.

We were about half a mile from the utility line. A Florence Water and Light representative told us we had to cut a strip 40 feet wide and a quarter-mile long through the woods so that the company could haul the poles in and string the wire. We also would need to get permission for the wire to cross private land. We also has to pay for the poles and the labor and hire a licensed electrician to install our wiring and connect it to the utility line. This bit deeply into our savings.

The next step was to try to dig a well. Talking this over with the people at Keyes Lake Grocery, we learned of a "water witch" who could find where the water came close to the surface of the ground. We contacted him. He came and crawled around on his hands and knees, dangling a quarter on a string in a glass of water. Suddenly the quarter started banging against the side of the glass.

"Wadder's 40 feet down," he said, "but there's enough to flood the whole county."

We paid him $50.00 and hired a well driller. When the driller finally came he had to go down 203 feet to find water. We almost cried when he presented the bill for the well and for installing the pump and lines into the house. It was more than we had payed for our land and hunting cabin, and three times as much as we had budgeted for it.

On October 31, I woke to hear Joan skrieking hysterically. "There is snow in the sink and all over the dishes and even on the bed covers!" she cried.

During the night two inches of snow had fallen, and some of it had blown in around the chimney and windows of the old cabin.

"Jim," my wife said, "we are not staying another night in this shack. Today we move. I don't care if the new place isn't ready."

By that night we had moved all the furniture and dishes into our new home. We are still living in it. It is as snug and comfortable as we had hoped, although we continued to finish the inside for several more years.

I had predicted before we moved to the north woods that we could get practically all of our meat from hunting and fishing. Now was the time to prove it, and for the first time we hunted and fished for food. We killed more than 100 snowshoe hares that first winter, and we ate them all. In the process we used or developed 27 recipes for cooking them.

When deer season came, Trapper and I each got a deer. We caught northern pike, bluegills and trout through the ice. During one period the fish were biting well for 21 days in a row. This hunting and fishing easily produced enough protein for our needs.

Trapper and I practically lived on meat and fish, even having venison steak and trout for breakfast.

"You have to be a caveman to eat rabbit every day," Jolain said, and she and Joan continued to eat about the same diet as they had before we moved to the north woods.

We had expected deep snow, and we were proved right. We plowed ourselves out until late February when we finally gave up and parked our pickup about half a mile away on a township road.

We hadn't had time to cut our winter's wood supply, so we cut it on a day-to-day basis. This was to get more difficult later after our chain saw broke. A few days after that our tractor broke down. From then on we cut our firewood with a hand saw and skidded it to the cabin on a toboggan. But even with our handpowered method of getting firewood, we still had plenty of time for hunting and fishing. What's more, we weren't spending money to get our fuel. So we got through the first winter. I believe it was the happiest time of my life. One day I told the family, "I feel like the luckiest guy in the world. I am doing exactly what I want to do."

Spring in the north woods is exciting and interesting. We actually got sunburned while standing in a snowbank that April when the temperature was less than 70 degrees. The ice on our pond turned from white to blue to black and finally splintered into thousands of chunks as a wall of water a foot high rushed down the creek leading into the pond. Soon robins, killdeers, meadow larks and blackbirds appeared in our woods and marsh, and ducks, geese and blue herons often showed up in a nearby pond. Almost a continuous chorus of bird songs emanated from the forest.

In late March we tapped maple trees and made several quarts of syrup from the sap. Soon green plants appeared and we made spring salad from the tender leaves of wild mustard, sorrel, violets, dandelions and new shoots of cattail. We also started clearing a patch of woods to use for a garden. Though the garden was only about 50 feet square, it supplied us with a surprising amount of food.

We worked like demons throughout the spring and summer, gardening and gathering foods. Every berry patch, wild cherry clump and feral apple tree was inspected and relieved of its bounty. I dug a root cellar behind the cabin, and we filled it with potatoes, apples, onions and other staples.

We also built a woodshed from slabs that could be had for the taking from a nearby sawmill, and we filled it with wood so that we wouldn't have to wade through snow to get fuel for our second winter. To have a firewood supply seemed to be a luxury.

We entered our second winter in the woods happy, secure and confident. Our experiment had succeeded. We were no longer making ourselves miserable while trying to be comfortable.

It's been eleven years now since we moved to the north woods, and we've never regreted it. I think that anybody else fed up with city life could escape to the woods as we have done. Money can be made in the backcountry by logging, driving a school bus, cutting Christmas trees and dozens of other full-tme and part-time jobs. I earn most of my income by writing for outdoor magazines and book publishers. Jim, Jr., who was 18 when we moved, made several hundred dollars that first winter by running a trapline. Our family has sold many wild medicinal herbs to drug companies. And good mechanics, plumbers and other tradesmen are as much in demand in rural areas as in the city.

If you want to take to the woods, I recommend that you first save enough cash to live on for the first year. We budgeted $10,000, which would have been plenty except for the extreme cost of our well. Because of inflation, you'd need much more than we had if you want to build a new house. But there are always ways to economize. For example, we could have cut down trees and could have had a sawmill cut them into lumber instead of buying lumber outright. That would have saved three quarters of the cost of our building.

I strongly suggest that you read every self-sufficiency book and magazine that you can find. Learn how to grow and preserve food, build a house, burn wood and so forth.

A great advantage of living in the woods is having the chance to hunt and fish a great deal. I hunt about 150 days a year and fish 60 days a year. And I haven't tired of it yet.

Probably the most important quality of a new homeland is that it has a climate you are accustomed to, or can readily adapt to. The entire section of North America north of a line stretched from Philadelphia to Reno, Nevada to the Arctic Circle has what is called a cool moist climate. Theoretically at least a person living in any part of this area could adapt quickly to any other part of it. Most people who live further south could also adapt within two years.

Don't forget that man can be acclimated in a year or two to extremes in temperature also. It was previously supposed that only Eskimos could live in the far frozen Arctic, but in late years whites, Orientals and black people have lived there for years on end.

Agreeably, the region covered by the cool moist climate includes most of the sparsely settled regions of the United States and Canada. Most people think that the further north they go, the colder it gets, and if we go strictly by the thermometer reading, it certainly is true. However, the ability of our environment to rob cold from our body is also influenced by the wind and humidity.

A good example of this happened the other day. After working outside all day on an addition to our cabin, I came inside and read the mail. I had a letter from my brother who lives in California. He mentioned that he had been trying to work outside but it got uncomfortably cool so he had to come inside. He wrote that it was about 30 degrees, but the wind was blowing hard. Our temperature was zero and it warmed up to about 20 degrees during the day. There was little wind, and I wasn't cold for one minute and got uncomfortably warm if I didn't pace myself. The difference was in the chill factor, the way we were dressed, and our individual thermostats, of course.

Humidity also is a factor in the comfort zone. The higher the humidity, the more cold seems to affect a human body. We frequently encounter temperature of 20 to 30 below zero in the north woods, but they don't seem as cold as when we lived further south with much warmer thermometer readings, but with a high wind and humidity. With proper clothing, the dry cold climate of the north is pleasant and invigorating.

A good selection of proper clothing will go a long way toward your comfort and efficiency in building a life in the woods.

Proper clothing is not only important in winter for protection from the cold, but also in other seasons for protection from insects, tree limbs, rain and even heat.

There is no shortage of information available to help the "Cabineer" select a proper wardrobe for backwoods living, but it is good to keep a few facts in mind. Down or a down substitute is the lightest material available that will keep you warm in any weather. However, be sure to obtain down garment that are covered with material tough enough for heavy wear in thick brush and while carrying wood, building cabins and fur trapping. Poplin or cotton/polyester or 1,000 denier nylon are some of the materials that are satisfactory. Rip-stop nylon and soft cotton outer shells will not withstand heavy wear.

Wool is fine material for wet and cool weather clothing. In a damp climate where frequent drizzle and light rain is prevalent, wool is much better than cotton or down clothing since it naturally sheds rain water and will retain heat even when wet. Wool trousers are the mainstay of outdoorsmen in the north in winter.

The trooper type of hat is the warmest style, chopper mittens with liners are much warmer than gloves, but they are still flexible enough to work with. Sorrel type boots with rubber bottoms and leather tops and felt liners are warm enough for any weather if a thick liner is used. In summer, tennis shoes are fine for backcountry wear, and waterproof leather boots answer for fall and spring wear.

Be sure to take tough, wear resistant work shirts and pants. Light duty clothing which would be satisfactory in the city might be worn out in one day of cutting wood or cabin building. I like blue jeans and sweatshirts, but if you don't mind the extra weight and stiffness, a work outfit made of cotton duck is much more wear resistant.

While you are getting ready to move you can select the type of cabin that you will want to build. The advantages of deciding this ahead of your move are many, but maybe the most help will result from actually building a scale model. By building a model you can figure exactly how much lumber or how many logs of a certain size you will need. You can plan the rooms and even decide what type of furniture you will build or take along.

Just as importantly, it will force you to look at the structure from all angles. You might not want a type or size of house after you actually look at a model of it. We live in an A frame cabin and like it well enough, but some people after looking decide they didn't want one, even though previously they did. They just weren't compatible with the slanting wall lines and narrow upstairs.

This will be a good time to decide if you can live without indoor plumbing, electric lights and running water also. Many people have moved far beyond the utility companies reach when they decided they didn't need electricity. In fact, they sought the independence of living without it. Then after living without electricity for a few months, the romance wore thin and they wished they had it.

Realize that in many areas you can build right on the edge of huge wooded, even wilderness areas with the finest hunting and fishing available and still be able to connect into the public utility. As hard as it is to realize until you investigate thoroughly, most utilities still furnish electricity cheaper than you can generate it yourself if all aspects are considered.

Wind generators and gasoline or propane fired generators are used with satisfaction in many areas, but if you expect to run a refrigerator, a dozen or more light bulbs, a freezer, a well pump motor, you need a good dependable high wattage unit and they are expensive to buy. Moreover, unless you live in an extremely windy place you will probably need a back up, gas fired generator, or an exceptionally large complex or nickel cadium storage batteries even if you have a good wind generator.

Too many people this is more trouble then it is worth, even if the huge expense is discounted. Nearly every appliance except a freezer will run on propane gas also, and except for the expense and the trouble of transporting the cylinders of gas it is an acceptable way of having these conveniences.

Solar cells that will generate enough electricity to keep a

large storage battery charged are also available. They are usually sold at camper supply outlets and are commonly used for charging batteries in motorhomes. They will keep a battery charged for running a television set and a few other appliances. Satellite television is available in the most remote locations.

Many people are satisfied with using a spring house or a nearby creek for a refrigerator. We built a log ice house on a remote homestead that we had and filled it with ice from the adjacent pond. It kept food very well all summer. In winter we had a "cold box" built into one wall of our cabin for keeping food cool. Naturally the northern winter weather solved our freezer problem in winter. For light we used an Alladin lamp. This type of lamp gives good light, but burns considerable fuel and it costs us nearly $1.00 a day to keep it in fuel.

Woodsmen who settle in wooded areas will have little trouble keeping warm since free firewood is available. Modern air tight heaters can deliver steady dependable heat with a minimum of wood. We heat our 1,200 square foot cabin with less than three cords of wood with a small air tight heater, and more often than not the temperature is higher than is recommended.

People with families are going to be concerned about educating their children. If you are not familiar with the rural education system you will probably be amazed at the distance that school buses range. Some up to 40 miles or more from the school. In fact, chances are if you settle along a good all weather road, the school will be required by law to send a bus for your children. Correspondence and satellite T.V. courses are available for children that absolutely cannot attend school. They are designed to be taught by the parent to the child and educators in Alaska have told me that home taught children often out score public school students on the three R's.

Many people when they are faced with making their own way worry immediately about how they will get enough food to eat. Yet food is all around us. Settle in an area where big game such as deer, elk, moose or caribou are available and you can satisfy all of your protein needs from these animals. Supplement them with fish and small game. Realize it only requires about half a pound of protein a day for each adult. In many areas this barely requires thinning the deer herd to its range carrying capacity each year.

Wild fruits and berries grow in all the green sections of the country, and they can be canned or frozen for year round use. If you live in a potato growing area, you can gather plenty of potatoes right from the fields in the fall and store them in a home built root cellar for year around use.

If you settle near a wheat or corn growing area, these grains will provide a base for your diet. Either grain can furnish a day's food need for about 25 cents if you grind the grain yourself. Indeed, even today it is possible to feed an adult for less than $2.00 a week if you are a skilled food forager, hunter and fisherman, and have potatoes, wheat or corn for a food base.

I have mentioned cost in the food discussion because almost everyone who writes to me to inquire about our lifestyles asks about how much money they should have before they take to the woods.

How much money this will be depends upon your personal plans. If you want to just move into the backcountry for a year or so of wilderness living, and you can make arrangements to stay in a temporary shelter, camper or empty cabin, you might get by with only a few thousand dollars. If you plan on a permanent move where you will be building a year around cabin, drilling a well and clearing land, the cost is going to be much higher. When we moved, we owned the land but had to build. Nevertheless we built our cabin and lived the first year on $10,000.00. However, the cost could be about 2-½ times that high nowadays.

Before you move or leave your present job, you should have the transportation, clothing, tools and books that you will need to succeed in your new life. Then money enough to carry you for the first year will all but guarantee that you will succeed.

I have been asked by would-be pioneers how they are supposed to save money when every dime they make goes to pay for the cost of the life they live now? But, everyone can save money. Cut out luxuries, sell the expensive car and take a second job. Ideally this second job will be one that will deliver experience that you can use in your new life. I knew a man who worked in a factory and cut firewood in his spare time. When the Arab oil embargo arrived and fuel prices shot sky high, his day arrived. He quickly moved north and began a firewood business that more then sustains his new lifestyle.

I spent more then four years of moonlighting before I could save enough money to move. But, every hour of the extra effort was well worth it. If you can't find a second job, develop a business of your own that you can take along. There are literally hundreds of small enterprises that are ignored by the large companies because they might only generate a few thousand dollars of income a year. Have three or four of these going and you might do well.

Who can take to the wilderness? You can if you want to. There is plenty of room and always will be in the backcountry for the special folks who need to breathe fresh air, forage their own food, live among trees and unspoiled lakes, watch the sunset over a wilderness horizon and hear the cry of a great horned owl or a lonesome wolf as darkess settles over your cabin clearing.

Chapter 2.

Finding Land For Your Cabin

Far and away the best state for young Americans who want to get away from it all, is the great land called Alaska. Only a tiny fraction of its 586,000 square miles of territory is settled, and no one knows what vast deposits of precious metals, rare stones and industrial resources are yet to be discovered in this gigantic state.

Some sections of Alaska have yet to be walked on by a white man, and alot of it is wilder than parts of America was when Paul Revere warned the Colonists that the British were coming. Yet a good road system reaches into many parts of Alaska to provide a jumping off place for deep bush living. In many places you can get a quarter of a mile off the paved road and be in utter wilderness where grizzly bear, moose and caribou are the chief inhabitants. Modern day pioneers can live as wild as they like and still have access to emergencies or supplies if they are needed.

Last summer we drove every paved road and many bush road in Alaska looking for lands suitable for cabin living. We estimated there was room for 50,000 bush dwellers with more then plenty of space between each one.

Of course, when you plan to subsist to a great extent off the land, you would do well to settle along a river that reaches the ocean. Then you can supplement moose steak and ptarmigan breast with 50 pound salmon. Some of the larger lakes also have good fish populations which are available the year around. Of course, a serviceable pickup or car which you might leave at a friend's place along the road system will transport you to a salmon river when they are running, if you don't settle on a river.

Literally thousands of cabin sites are available along the ocean also, or on islands. A good example of this territory is southern Alaska which extends nearly 400 miles south from Haines between Canada and the Pacific Ocean. About 125 miles wide, the "panhandle" is made up of numerous islands and a relatively thin stretch of rugged mainland.

Warmed by balmy ocean currents, the panhandle has the mildest temperature in Alaska. Temperatures in some areas seldom get below freezing, even in January, and almost never drop below 10 degrees. Summers also are temperate, with 60 to 70 degrees commonly expected. However, it also has the highest precipitation of all areas of Alaska with the populated areas receiving from 80 to 200 inches of precipitation annually. Winters alternate between snow, rain and sunshine so the snow accumulation is usually minimal.

The only towns in the panhandle that are accessible by road are Skagway and Haines in the northern section and Hyder in the southern part. The rest of this enchanted land of towering spruce, waterfalls, and stunning seascapes is accessible by a rapid system of ocean ferries.

Besides remote and unspoiled islands that seem to beckon to the cabin dweller are the hundreds of miles of coastline that seem made to order for a family that wants to live on a boat. Imagine a life where you fish for trout and salmon in the morning, tend shrimp and crab pots in the afternoon and hunt brown bear or moose in the evening. This is available in the panhandle if you can arrange to buy or build a boat that can survive the mild seas found in the inland passage. Numerous ports and protected bays offer a haven from any storm that might sweep across the ocean.

Almost all of the southeastern Alaska lies within the Tongass National Forest which incidently is the largest national forest in the United States. Approximately 54,000 people live in the panhandle, about 1/5 are Tlingiy, Haida and Tsimshian Indians. 75 percent of the whites live in the towns of Juneau, Petersburg, Wrangell, Ketchikan and Sitka.

Most of the people make a living from fishing and fish processing, lumbering and government. Tourism is also a major source of income. Whales, sealions and porpoises are frequently sighted from shore, and deer, moose, black and brown bear and furbearing animals are hunted or trapped in the southeast.

Most of the species of trout and salmon as well as salt water fish are caught by sports fishermen. Many of the rivers on the mainland and on Prince Of Wales Island have excellent steelhead runs as well as pink, red, silver and dog salmon runs.

Perhaps the largest concentration of bald eagles in the world is found in southeast Alaska. More than 20,000 have been counted, and one observer reports 40 eagles sitting on a single tree limb.

Each settlement in the panhandle is different from the rest, and the new settler probably should take time to examine each one, perhaps by traveling on the system of government ferries, they stop at each town six days a week, going both north and south.

The southern-most town is Ketchikan. Located on Reveillagigedo Island, this city lies 600 miles north of Seattle, Washington. With a population of 11,737 in the borough, Ketchikan is the southeasts fifth largest city. Ketchikan keeps two shopping centers in operation as well as supplying the work force for two salmon canneries, a pulp mill and a sawmill. It is a narrow city built on the side of a mountain. Its waterfront runs for several miles, and it is the site of constant activity as the seaplanes and boats move in and out of the harbor.

Ketchikan's climate is mild with an average winter temperature of 33 degrees and an average July temperature of 53 degrees. Average precipitation is 164 inches, but during the month of November in 1969, a whopping 43 inches of rain deluged the area.

About 45 miles west of Ketchikan lies Prince of Wales Island, the third largest island that flies the American flag. Measuring about 125 miles (north-south) by 45 miles (east-west). Prince of Wales Island is a heavily wooded island with low mountains. There are four major communities on the huge island, and many small fishing and logging camps. A fair road system allows travel to many parts of the island.

The island offers inland fishing for four species of salmon as well as steel head and Dolly Varden trout. Black bear, deer, beaver, wolf, mink, marten and river otter are found on the island.

The town of Wrangell lies 85 miles north of Ketchikan on Wrangell Island. Population of Wrangell is 2,345 and most of the people work at the Alaska Lumber and Pulp Company or in the fishing industry. Wrangell is slightly drier than other panhandle communities with an annual average precipitation of about 80 inches. Its strategic location at the mouth of the brawling and lengthy Sitikine River made it a prime site for fur traders and gold seekers in frontier days.

The next town the north bound traveler would discover is Petersburg with 3,001 residents. Located about 120 air miles north of Ketchikan, Petersburg has about 105 inches of precipitation annually. Petersburg has a strong Norwegian heritage as many of the people are descended from Norwegian fishermen. Most of the people work in the bustling fishing industry where salmon, herring, crab and halibut are caught and processed.

Sitka has a population of 7,297 people, and lies 185 air miles north of Ketchikan. Formerly the capitol of Russian Alaska, Sitka was once called the Paris of the Pacific. It boasted flour mills, sawmills, shipyards and tanneries. However, now most of the modern residents work at logging or fishing or for the Forest Service.

Sitka is quite probably the most scenic of the southeast towns. It is surrounded by deep water capes and snowcapped mountains. It also has an extinct volcano and historic and unusual buildings. The climate is drier than some southeastern communities with about 82 total inches of precipitation, with snow on the ground being an unusual sight.

Juneau is the capitol of Alaska, and it is the southern most city to be located on the mainland. The population of the city and borough is 22,680, and most people work at lumbering, fishing, tourism or for the government, with government being at present the largest employer. The climate is typical of southeastern Alaska, but it has some snowfall on the ground intermittently between mid-November and mid-April. Juneau has the most extensive road system of any of the cities discussed so far, and resident glaciers.

Haines and Skagway are both located on the mainland, and both are connected to road systems. Although they have relatively mild temperatures both summer and winter, they receive much less rainfall than the rest of the panhandle communities. This brief description of the southeastern communities will help the modern day pioneer decide which areas to investigate in a search for a cabin site or semi-permanent boat mooring location.

However, the southeastern section is only one of the five sections of Alaska. Traveling north, the next section is called south central Alaska. This includes the famed Kenai Peninsula, where good roads, mild climate, fishing, clamming and big game hunting is productive and in reach of everyone. Known as the playground of Anchorage, the Kenai nevertheless contains territory that is wild enough to satisfy most. The largest moose in the world live on the Kenai Peninsula as well as the biggest bears, and some say the biggest salmon.

The modern bustling city of Anchorage now has more than 125,000 people as well as high rise office buildings and fast food stores. A few miles of Anchorage, the town of Palmer, sits in the well known Manatuska Valley, where huge vegetables and dairy cattle are a common sight. Here the climate is milder than most northern 48 states, and if a cabin site is found in the nearby forest, wild game can be supplemented with the output of a garden patch.

Along the coast, south of the Kenai Peninsula, the Prince William Sound territory included miles of beautiful coastline teeming with wildlife and waters rich with fish and shellfish.

The town of Valdez, which is the southern end of the Alaska pipeline is the only main settlement connected to the road system. The town of Cordova, also on Prince William Sound must be reached by boat or by air. Whittier can be reached by rail. Between these widely separated population centers are hundreds of miles of spectacular unsettled cabin country.

South central Alaska, unlike southeast, has most of the convenience of mainland transportation plus access to the Pacific Ocean for reaping its bounty. Generally speaking, the climate is much drier without being too much colder. Several salmon rivers extend far inland.

Interior Alaska has more land for the settling than will be used in the lifetime of anyone alive today. It has far more moose, caribou, sheep and bear than people. Unlike the almost vertical southeast and south central, the interior has flat or rolling lands that reach as far as the eye can see, with probably a scenic mountain range in the background.

The chief outfitting center is the town of Fairbanks with about 50,000 people. This is a center for trappers, prospectors, oil workers and loggers, as well as participants of less strenuous occupations. Other outfitting centers in the interior are Tok, North Pole, Big Delta and Fort Yukon. All of these towns are surrounded by sheer wilderness.

The climate in the interior is dry. Fairbanks only has 11 inches of precipitation per year, including about 65 inches of snow. The interior has hot short summers and long cold winters. In summer the temperature can reach 90 degrees or more, and in winter it can drop to 60 degrees below zero.

In June and July there are 21 hours of full daylight and about three hours of twilight, so it never really gets dark. In winter the long nights are illuminated by starlight and the Aurora Borealis, so it is possible to travel on foot, without lights across the snow.

Log cabin dwellers live high on moose steaks and Dall sheep roast during the winter while they trap, ice fish, or snowshoe through the hushed wilderness.

Major rivers which are filled with five kinds of salmon during the spawning season, cut through the interior. Rainbow,

brook and cut throat trout, as well as Arctic grayling and Doly
Varden are also catchable. Northern pike and sheefish are
plentiful but often overlooked.

The mighty Yukon River winds through the territory on its
way to the Bering Sea. Generally called the fourth largest river
in the world, the Yukon drains 330,000 square miles, an area
as large as France and Poland combined. In some places it is
20 miles wide and in some places a mere mile wide. Many native
villages are found along the banks, and the towns of Eagle and
Circle separated by 160 miles of river are rich in history and
offer a settler a jumping off place along the river.

The southeast, south central and interior Alaska have most
of the population, and all are connected at least partly to the
road system, even though the southeast has only two towns with
road connections.

Southwest Alaska contains the famed Kodiak Island and
Kodiak Island chain, as well as the game rich Alaska Peninsula,
and the Aleutian Islands. Kodiak Island has military bases and
about 5,000 inhabitants. Here are the largest brown bears in the
world as well as Sitka deer and mountain goat. The offshore
waters teem with salmon and halibut and three species of crabs.
Kodiak Island is world famous as a seafood processing and ship-
ping center.

On nearby Afognak and Raspberry Islands live the only herd
of elk in Alaska, as well as deer, bear and ptarmigan. The main
drawback to living on the Kodiak Island is the unpredictable
blustery weather and high cost of living.

The Alaskan Peninsula offers some of the finest hunting
in Alaska for brown bear, moose and caribou. The offshore
waters teem with salmon, and inland lakes and rivers offer good
trout fishing. The huge inland Illimiana Lake is also a fine
fishing spot if you have a boat. Settle on this peninsula and
except during the hunting season you certainly won't be bother-
ed by men or his confusion, while you watch whales, porpoises,
seals, sealions and sea otters cavort in the waves.

Towns in the area are King Salmon, Kanatak, Illiamana and
Chignik. All have airports and are useful for jumping off places.
King Salmon has a post office.

Bethel and Nome, each with a population of about 4,000 people, are the largest settlements facing the Bering Sea. Bethel is the largest town in western Alaska and is a bustling community with its own hospital, police and community college. It's salmon fishing industry is worth 5 million dollars a year, and private industry employs many people year round. It is a hub city for 52 villages spread out around Bethel in a region as large as Oregon.

Nome has been "legendized" in song and poem for the last century. This is the town where Will Rogers and Wiley Post crashed their plane in 1935 with fatal results to both. Accessible only by air during most of the year, Nome nevertheless is the oldest city in Alaska, and has the oldest first class school district. Its front street is located so close to the Bering Sea that boulders are piled along the waterfront to prevent waves from damaging the buildings during a storm, as happened in 1974.

It is the trading center for several surrounding Eskimo villages, and even has a short road system that is maintained in summer. The blueberry crop is reputed to be world famous.

Besides the areas mentioned, the region along the Bering Sea between the Alaska range on the south and the Seward Peninsula on the north is Eskimo land. Here in a vast untamed land of polar bears and walrus, Eskimo still carve ivory and harpoon whales from skin boats as they have for centuries. However, the igloo is about gone now except for overnight stops, and many natives live in frame houses with running water and even flush toilets. Satellite T.V. beamed into many homes and airplanes land and take off regularly when the unpredictable weather is agreeable.

North of the Arctic Circle (but including the Brooks Range) the region north of the Arctic Ocean is called Arctic Alaska. This also is mostly popluated by Eskimos, although the Dalton Highway or "haul road" follow the pipeline to Prudhoe Bay, making it possible to drive from Fairbanks clear to the Arctic Ocean. A vast caribou herd travels this territory, and in some places a hunter can bag five animals if he wants. Moose also are available in this region, especially for local cabin dwellers. The regulations restrict sport hunting to some degree in Arctic

Alaska, but Dall sheep, grouse, ptarmigan and waterfowl, bears, wolves and foxes are available to the inhabitants of these sections. Grayling, Dolly Varden, burbot, whitefish and pike are available to fishermen in the inland waters, while Arctic Ocean tributaries are good places to catch sea going fish.

The town of Kotezebue, with a population of about 2,000 is 80% Eskimo. Located in Kotezebue Sound, on the Baldwin Peninsula of the Bering Sea, it is headquarters for ten surrounding villages scattered over a 43,000 square mile area.

In Arctic Alaska along the Yukon River near the confluence of the Porcupine and Yukon is the settlement of Fort Yukon. With a population of 612, Fort Yukon is headquarters for the Yukon Flats area. It has a state trooper's office and a Fish and Game headquarters. It is a chief jumping off place for the game rich surroundings.

The state of Alaska has several aggressive plans for transferring land from state ownership to private hands. Almost anyone who has lived in Alaska for 12 months is eligible to buy or acquire these lands. Some are agricultural lands and some are designed for homes or cabin sites.

The following is a direct quote from an official state land disposal brochure.

"The Alaska Department of Natural Resources regularly makes lands available for private ownership to Alaskans through the lottery, homesite, homestead and public auction programs. To acquire land under these programs, persons must be 18 years of age and with the exception of auctions, have been an Alaskan resident for at least 12 months prior to application. The Department regularly holds one major land disposal offering each year. This offering consists of a mixture of land programs and generally requires the interested individual to file an application to purchase the land. If more than one application is received for any one parcel, a lottery or drawing is held to award the parcel winner. Land not awarded at these drawings is usually made available over the counter under the same terms and conditions as the original offering. The filing period for the Summer 1985 State Land Disposal offering is 8:00 A.M., May 13, 1985 through 4:30 P.M., July 12, 1985.

Applications must be actually, physically received by the Division Of Land And Water Management on or before that deadline."

Complete information on land currently listed for disposal and lands that will be listed for disposal in the future can be obtained from anyone of the eight Division Of Land And Water Management regional offices. Write the Department Of Natural Resources, Division Of Land And Water Management, Pouch 7-005, Anchorage, Alaska 99510, for lands in the south central; Department Of Natrual Resources, Department Of Land And Water, Willoughby, Suite 400, Juneau, Alaska 99811, Department Of Natural Resources, Department Of Land And Water, Pouch MA, Juneau, Alaska, for lands in the southeast; Department Of Natural Resources, Department Of Land And Water, O. L&W M, 4420 Airport Way, Fairbanks, Alaska 99701, for lands in the northern region.

The homesteading programs and the remote cabin site long time lease programs will be of particular interest to the readers of this book. See the chart, Alaska State Lands Program, for complete information. **See the following listing for other information about Alaska.**

Farmers Home Administration: P.O.Box 1289, Palmer, Alaska 99645 (745-2176). Provides loans and technical assistance on residential development and rural renewal programs and farm loan programs. Grant/loan program on public works projects including water and sewer.

The Alaska Railroad: Box 7-2111, Anchorage, Alaska 99510 (265-2411). Owned by the United States government and operated by the Department of Transportation, the railroad provides 482 miles of main line track from the ice free ports of Sewart and Whittier, through Anchorage to Fairbanks. For schedules and fares, call Anchorage (265-2490).

Commercial Fisheries Entry Commission (CFEC): Pouch KB, Juneau, Alaska 99811 (586-3456). State commerical fisheries licensing entry permit interim use permit and vessel license renewal/issuance.

National Marine Fisheries Service; Box 1668, Juneau, Alaska 99802 (586-7223). Federal vessel loans, exploratory fishing, gear development, basic biological and oceanographic research on marine resources, seafood processing technology information and fur seal management assistance.

U.S. Fish and Wildlife Service, Alaska Regional Office: 1011 East Tudor Road, Anchorage, Alaska 99503 (562-2271). Manages wildlife refuges, protection of marine manual and migritory birds and applied wildlife research. Technical fishing management assistance.

Alaska Department Of Fish And Game: P.O. Box 3-20000 Juneau, Alaska 99802 (465-4100). State development and conservation of commercial fisheries, sport fish, bird, game and fur bearing animals, fishing and hunting opportunities.

Cooperative Extension Service, University of Alaska: 1514 W. Cushman, Room 303, Fairbanks, Alaska 99701 (452-1548). State rural community development organizational activities, farm management information, homemakers, 4-H farmers organizational work and publications of specific practical Alaskan oriented agricultural information.

Newspapers

The Nome Nugget
P.O. Box 619
Nome, Alaska 99762

Fairbanks Daily News-Miner
P.O. Box 710
Fairbanks, Alaska 99707

Anchorage Daily News
200 Potter Drive
Anchorage, Alaska 99501

Pioneer Printing Co.
Ketchikan Daily News
Southeastern Log
P.O. Box 7900
Ketchikan, Alaska 99901

Where to write for more information in Alaska:

Alaska Travel Division
Pouch E
Juneau, Alaska 99801
(Tours, roads and accomadations)

Department of Highways
Box 1467
Juneau, Alaska 99801
(Road conditions, maps, jobs)

Department of Public Works
Division of Marine Transportation
Box 1361
Juneau, Alaska 99801
(Ferry schedules)

Bureau of Land Management
701 C Box 13
Anchorage, Alaska 99513

National Park Service
Alaska Area Office
540 W. 5th
Anchorage, Alaska 99501

U.S. Forest Service
Box 1628
Juneau, Alaska 99802

Bureau of Sport Fisheries and
   Wildlife
1011 E. Tudor Road
Anchorage, Alaska 99503

Alaska Department of
   Transportation and Public
   Facilities
Pouch Z
Juneau, Alaska 99811

Wild Lands In The "Lower 48"

Although Alaska and the Canadian provinces are what most people think of when they start laying plans for taking to the woods, the truth is, there are many areas in the Lower 48 that are wild enough for almost anyone.

Even in the east, the state of Maine has vast areas where the human population is sparse and the forests reach to the horizon and beyond. Nearly anywhere north of a line drawn from Rangeley to Lincoln, Maine is a possibility for cabin living. In fact, in some places that I have been in Maine, the big game animals outnumber the human population.

Most of the large wilderness areas are owned by private concerns, but there are cabin lands on the fringe of these sections that would gladden the heart of the modern day pioneer. My choice for a homestead location in Maine would be in the Moosehead Lake country. Here deer, bear, moose and small game are common, and trout as long as your arm are brought to the net.

Respectable mountains reach towards the sky, and not too many miles to the east, the Atlantic Ocean waits for clam diggers, lobster fishermen and deep sea anglers.

The three upper midwestern states also are worth considering. The state of Michigan is densely populated in the southern section, but if you cross the Straits of Mackinac and enter the Upper Peninsula, the surroundings change completely. Here miles and miles of woods and water are broken only by an occasional hamlet and a few large towns.

The entire northern border of the Upper Peninsula is formed by three Great Lakes. There are far more varieties of salmon and trout in the Great Lakes now than when Columbus discovered America. Deer, bear and a budding moose herd make up the big game animal population and small game is abundant.

Cabin lands are plentiful and inexpendable. Many are located far back in the bush where a refugee from the urban life could live out the rest of his days in utter solitude if he wished.

Bordering Michigan, is northern Wisconsin. North of Highway #8, which stretches from Pembine on the east to Hudson on the west are about 20,000 square miles of mostly forested and wild land. I make my home in this territory, and I can walk out my back door and keep walking for hundreds of miles without coming out of the woods, if I wished. I can fish streams that are seldom fished by anyone else and hunt without ever encountering another hunter.

Wisconsin has one of the largest deer herds in the nation, and black bear are common. Snowshoe hare are so thick that there is no need to ever close the season, and ruffed grouse inhabit nearly every thicket. Two Great Lakes offer salmon and trout fishing, and thousands of inland lakes and streams make fishing within easy reach of anyone.

Most of the northern counties have lands that they dispose of on a regular basis, and there is a brisk trade in the sale of hunting cabins and wooded homesites among realtors and private sales.

Most of what has been said about Michigan and Wisconsin is also true of Minnesota, but Minnesota has even more wild land and larger unbroken forests. In addition, the largest timber wolf pack south of Alaska sings it's mournful but thrilling song in the northeastern regions of the Gopher State.

Minnesota also has a huntable moose herd. At this time the land prices in the northern parts of Minnesota are even lower than they are in Michigan and Wisconsin, and that makes them a good bargain indeed.

At least four of the western states also can offer solitude, excellent hunting and fishing, and available land for building. Montana has over 145,000 square miles of land and only ¾ million people. Most of the wilderness lands are in the western part, with the northwestern being particularly scenic and unspoiled. Towns that are located near wild areas are Kalispell, Hamilton, Dillion and Cutbank. Montana's big game hunting and fishing are world famous.

Wyoming has an even lower population of people. Indeed, the antelope herd is larger than the human population. Deer, elk, bear and small game also are plentiful, as well as some of the best inland fishing in the nation.

The Big Horn Mountains and foothills west of the town of Sheridan has some excellent areas for the "cabineer", as does the entire northwestern section of Wyoming, from the town of Pinedale, north to Yellowstone National Park.

I have hunted in the Bridger Teton National Forest and backpacked in the Tetons and can attest that this land is about as wild as it was when Columbus discovered America.

Another remote and colorful section of Wyoming is located in the Bear Lake country, where the borders of Idaho, Wyoming and Utah join. Some towns that are outfitting centers for particularly wild areas are Cody, Pinedale, Dubois, Lander and Sheridan.

The state of Idaho and Washington also offer many possibilities for the woodsman. The panhandle of Idaho is the most sparsely populated and has the most public land of any sections of Idaho. All the common species of big game are found in the panhandle, including a few woodland caribou.

Almost all of eastern Idaho, north of the town of Challis to the Canadian border is wild, mountainous lands. Plenty of room to roam for a lifetime where bear and elk far outnumber the human population. Most of this land is in national forest and can't be built upon, but this still leaves a few hundred miles of fringe areas where it is legal to build a cabin. Strategically located towns include Challis, Pierce and Sandpoint.

Washington state is more heavily settled, but still offers hundreds of square miles of rugged backcountry along the Idaho border, and in the Cascade Mountain range. Washington also has some stretches of remote Pacific Ocean seacoast for woodsmen who like to settle where they can gather seafood to supplement the elk and deer steaks. Towns where information can probably be obtained are, Bend, Hoodriver, Oakridge and Mazama.

Cabin Lands In Canada British Columbia

Stretching between the "Lower 48" states and the Alaska panhandle is the magnificent province of British Columbia. Within its borders is hundreds of miles of remote Pacific Ocean coastline, gigantic mountain reaches and rushing rivers. Its climate varies from rainy, warm weather along the coast to cold, dry weather east of the coastal mountain ranges. British Columbia has 118,000,000 acres of forested lands, more than any state or province.

From Powell River north to Stewart stretch a lush coastline with the coastal mountain range in the background. Inlets and fiords reach for dozens of miles inland to provide a safe harbor for a small but seaworthy boat while the pioneer family live high on salmon, moose, bear, deer, elk and mountain sheep.

Besides the mainland coastline, the beautiful Queen Charlott Islands are remote with deep bays and inlets and rich ocean fish, shell fish, Sitka deer and huge black bear. It seldom, if ever, freezes along the coast, and growing seasons last for all 12 months of the year, with about 250 frost free days. Fish found in this area include Dolly Varden, steelhead and salmon.

Towns north of Vancouver, along the coast, with connections to the road systems are, Bella Coola, Prince Rupert, Stewart and Greenville, although the latter can only be reached by a restricted road. From Bella Coola, Highway #20 reaches east for about 300 miles to the city of Williams Lake and connects to the high speed Caribou Highway.

The Yellowhead and Cassiar Highways were built through

west central and northwest British Columbia, some of the most scenic and unspoiled regions left on earth. Passing through more than 1,000 miles of mountains, unbroken forests dotted with unbelievably appealing lakes and wild rivers. These road systems have to be driven to be believed.

Another section of British Columbia with unlimited possibilities is the Atlin district which lies between the Yukon and the Alaskan coast. Highways #3, #7, and the Klondike Road reach south from the Alaskan Highway into this district.

Cabin lands are plentiful either directly along these road systems or on the sideroads that lead into the bush. The prospective settler should traverse this road system and look the country over very carefully. Stop at the little towns along the way and talk it over with the local people. Every village has an official or unofficial spokesman who can point the visitor in the right direction to assess the possibilities available in the region.

After you find the place you want to settle in, consult the government agencies at the addresses listed at the end of this section or inquire of the local officials to find out if the lands can be purchased or leased.

Ministry of Lands
Parks And Outdoor Recreation
    Department
1019 Wharf Street
Victoria, British Columbia U8U1X4

Fish and Wildlife Branch
Ministry of Environment
Parliment Buildings
Victoria, British Columbia U8U1X4

You must become a Canadian citizen to homestead land in British Columbia. Anyone can apply for citizenship, and to start this procedure write to:

Canadian Immigration Office
1550 Albernie Street
Vancouver, British Columbia
    V6G1A3
Phone 604-666-2171

Yukon Territory

The very name, Yukon Territory, brings a thrill to the breast of people who have the spirit of adventure. And I can attest, it lives up to its reputation. Towering snow covered mountain peaks look down on ice blue lakes and the majestic Yukon River. Moose, three kinds of bear, caribou and mountain sheep supply the few inhabitants with all the steaks and chops they want. But, if they tire of big game, ptarmigan, five kinds of grouse and numerous waterfowl will offer a variety of food. Arctic grayling, three species of salmon and trout will make sure the fish plate is filled, and many residents net whitefish just for their dogs to eat.

Most of the Yukon is forested. Lodge pole pine and spruce are well distributed and both species grow tall and symetrical, and provide good logs for building cabins. Edible wild plants and flowers carpet thousands of acres in season. In summer it never gets dark and in winter the short days are lighted by clear star filled skies that make foot and dog team travel possible, even after the sun sets.

At present there are more then 10 square miles of territory for each inhabitant, and half of those live in or very close to Whitehorse, while most of the rest live in the vicinity of Dawson, Watson Lake and Mayo.

The Yukon is mostly wide open to living the adventurous life for the hearty and dedicated cabineer. Wild, unspoiled lands lie close to the population centers, and there is no need to get so far away from emergency help that you run undue risks. Almost everything the remote wilderness has to offer is found within 50 miles of the largest towns in the Yukon.

Fish and Game Information
   Headquarters
Wildlife and Parks
Whitehorse District Office
Building 271, Marwell Area
P.O. Box 2703
Whitehorse, Yukon Y1A2C6

Available lands, business opportunities and jobs

Department of Economic
   Development and Tourism
Government of Yukon
Box 2703
Whitehorse, Yukon Y1A2C6

For Immigration Offices

Canadian Immigration Office
Room 101, Federal Building
308 Main Street
Whitehorse, Yukon, Canada Y1A2B5
Phone 403-667-5010

Northwest Territory

The Northwest Territory has 1,253,000 square miles of territory and only 50,000 people. This means the Northwest Territory is as large as Texas, Alaska, California and New Mexico combined, and has hardly enough people to populate a city. Almost all of the Canadian Eskimos (Inuits) live in the Northwest Territory, and it also has a sizeable population of Dena and Metis Indians. The white population is about equal to the Indian and Eskimo population combined.

Most of the white people live in or near the towns of Yellow Knife, Hay River, Fort Smith and Fort Simpson. Yellow Knife has about 10,000 people, and is the only city in the Territory. It is also the capitol. Most work in government, mining or oil and gas exploration or in transportation. Many of the Eskimos and Indians live off the land, and they have for centuries. However, they have modern guns and boats to aid their endeavors. They also make and sell native arts and crafts. Tourism is increasing in importance as more and better transportation becomes available.

The climate ranges from the hot dry, but short summer, when the temperature can go to 80 degrees and winters when temperatures can plunge to 60 degrees below zero or lower. However, the low humidity mitigates the psychological effect of the temperature extremes, and most people find the climate more invigorating than deadening.

The Northwest Territory includes all of far northern Canada, except the Yukon. The Territory has over 51,000 square miles of fresh water contained in over 100,000 lakes, and myraid of rivers and streams. This makes the area a haven for fish and waterfowl.

All the big game animals common to the Yukon are also found in the Northwest Territory and the big game population includes the gigantic procupine caribou herd. This herd is estimated to contain more than 110,000 animals and reaches from horizon to horizon when it is on the move. Northwest Territory also has a sizeable buffalo herd.

Northwest Territory includes the Barren Lands, a vast territory north of the tree line. The Barren Lands sweep north to the Hudson's Bay and the Arctic Ocean. A gigantic archipelago made up of islands as large as states, jut from the Beaufort Sea and the Arctic Ocean north of the mainland of the Territory. Here Eskimos hunt polar bear, seal and walrus as a matter of everyday survival.

It also includes the sprawling miles wide Mackenzie River, often called the Mississippi of the north because it flows for almost 1,200 miles from the Great Slave Lake to the Beaufort Sea and drains more the ¾ million acres.

Great Slave Lake and the Mackenzie River valley have a long enough growing season so vegetables, grain and hay can be raised, sometimes with outstanding success. The perpetual daylight in summer combined with up to 100 frost free days speeds the growth of potatoes, tomatoes, berries and even some fruit trees. Onion, cabbage, radishes and other vegetables are often quite successfully raised.

Good road systems reach into the Territory. Highway #3 or Mackenzie Highway, which extends from Alberta to Yellow Knife. This road crosses the Mackenzie River via a ferry. In spring when the ice is thawing and at the onset of winter when the ice is freezing, the road is closed and travel into Yellow Knife is by aircraft only. When the ice freezes solid, the road crosses the Mackenzie on the ice bridge.

Another road system is the Highway #8 or Dempster Highway. It reaches from Dawson, Yukon to Fort McPherson and Inuvik. The Dempster extends for about 446 miles through some of the most remote territory on the North American Continent. It is the only public highway that crosses the Arctic Circle.

The Dempster traverses country that changes from rolling hills, encircling clear streams and rivers to Arctic tundra. Dall sheep, grizzly bear and ptarmigan are common along the Dempster, and the gigantic porcupine caribou herd often migrate near the highway on its way to or from the Alaksa coast where it spends the summer.

Both Fort McPherson and Inuvik are thriving towns where the people work for the government, in mining or hunt, trap and fish for a living. Fort McPherson is located in one of the best muskrat and mink trapping areas to be found in the Territory.

The newest road system is the Liard Highway which reaches from Fort Nelson, British Columbia to Fort Simpson. Routes branch from the main highways to Fort Resolution, Pine Point and Fort Smith. These highways are well maintained gravel roads with free government operating ferries at the river crossing.

There is plenty of room for the "cabineer" in the Northwest Territory, and there probably will be for decades to come. However, some restrictions on harvesting the renewable resources are placed on non-natives and this should be taken into account. Contact the Department of Information at the end of the chapter for information about available lands, game and fish, or jobs or businesses.

Department of Information
Government of the Northwest
    Territory
Yellow Knife, Northwest Territory,
    Canada
Phone 403-873-7556

Figure 1.   There are a surprising number of occupations that take place in the backcountry. Here a forestry crew erect a sign on a national forest.

Chapter 3.

Make Money In The Woods

As clever at improvising as you might be, and as willing to sacrifice, you are still going to need some source of income. This doesn't have to be large. We have found that we can make one dollar do the work of $10.00 by being as self-sufficient as possible, and being very clever about how and where we spend that dollar. We have already discussed getting food as economically as possible. Tools can be purchased from farm, household and business bankruptcy auctions at very little cost. Clothes can be home sewn or bought at flea markets, Salvation Army and garage sales. A "mechanics special" snowmobile, boat motor or pickup truck can be purchased for low cost and rebuilt at home. But, still the bottom line is that you are going to need some income. Here's how to get it.

Since the mid 1960's, fur trapping has been a very good way for rural people to make an income. Fur trapping has gone through cycles where the income to be derived from it ranges from excellent to poor. In the early 1920's, trapping was a very good way to make an independent income. Many made a good yearly wage. This dropped off after World War

II, and fur prices were very low from the late 1940's until mid 1960.

At the present time, fur prices, while not at their spectacular high of a few years ago, nevertheless is still good enough to reward a cabineer with enough income to carry him until the next season. This is contingent on the fur bearer populations, the seasons, how many other trappers there are to compete with, and the trappers own skill and industry. Luck also plays a part.

In Canada, trap lines are registered, and it is illegal to trap on another person's line. In the United States, including Alaska, no such regulation exists. However, considerable friction develops when new trappers move in on an established line, and when you move into new territory and plan on establishing a trapline, it is well to get to know the resident trappers and discuss with them the places that you plan on trapping. Chances are, in most remote territory, there will be plenty of room for you to trap without incurring the animosity of trappers who are already there.

The most profitable animals to trap are muskrats, mink, raccoon and beaver in most areas. Other animals that can yield a good income, depending upon their populations, are fox, coyotes, bobcat, lynx, marten and fisher. Red squirrels in the far north provide income to some trappers, as do weasel and miscellaneous animals such as skunk.

The muskrat has been called the trappers meal ticket, and for good reason. He is considered an easy animal to catch, the price is unually fair enough to yield good wages for the time spent, and the equipment needed to trap muskrats is low in cost compared to some other animals, such as coyote and fox.

The beginner starting out to trap muskrats will need at least three dozen #1 traps. If the budget will allow, be sure to buy the stop loss type of trap that will prevent wring offs. They will pay for themselves several times over in greater catches. If you anticipate trapping raccoon with the same traps as you will be using for muskrats, then get #1-½ long spring traps, since they will be used for each. But, more about raccoon trapping later.

You will also need a pair of hip boots or chest waders, and

Figure 2. Wildlife workers prepare to blast a beaver dam to allow the water to flow. The beavers had created a pond that threatened the highway.

if possible, a Jon boat or canoe. In most areas the lakes will have a resident muskrat population. Rivers are even better because most have sloughs and marshes along their banks, which will provide a haven for muskrats.

You will also need at least one dozen muskrat stretches, but they can be made from low cost paneling or other thin boards if you don't want to buy wire stretchers. Wire stretchers dry the fur in shorter time and are more expedient.

You will need a pack basket for carrying traps, a small hatchet for cutting and driving stakes, a coil of trap wire and a pair of pliers.

Muskrat colonies are easy to recognize because of the dome shaped houses that 'rats live in. Other sign will be feed beds and bank holes, with usually some peeled roots or stalks of plants floating in the entrance. They also have 'runs" or trails coming out of the water and upon the bank where they go looking for plants on the land.

Feed beds look like small rafts of floating vegetation, and they usually contain a maze of roots or plant fibers that the 'rat has eaten the edible parts of and discarded the rest. "Rats make these floating feed beds as places to rest while they are eating.

Place your trap on the feed bed and use a long enough stake so the trap can be staked to the bottom of the lake independent of the feed bed. When the 'rat is caught, he will leap off the feed bed and quickly drown.

The 'rat houses also are good places to set a trap. Usually around the base of the house will be a flat area where the 'rat rests while eating or basking in the sun. Set the trap on these flat areas. Again, stake the trap down so the stake is independent of the 'rat house, and in deep enough water so the 'rat will drown. This requires about 1 foot of water. Traps set in the entrance of holes and in the runs are set in the water at the entrance. They also should be staked so the 'rats will drown.

'Rat traps are tended everyday. During the first two days if the traps are set right you will catch about ½ the 'rats in the marsh. The next three days you will catch about 1/3 of the

Figure 3.   A snowmobile is important to the trapper since it allows him to transport heavy loads for long distances in a short time.

remaining 'rats. Then it is time to pull the traps since you don't want to catch so many that you kill the breeding population.

After the 'rats are caught, usually they are laid out in the sun and air so the hair dries before they are skinned.

Muskrats are about the easiests fur animal to skin. In fact, some champion type skinners can strip the hide from a muskrat in 15 seconds. This is the method usually used. Grasp the muskrat by a hind leg and straighten it out so the weight is hanging from the leg. This pulls the skin tight so you can insert the point of the knife under the heel just above the black skin of the foot. Using a sharp knife with a skinning blade, cut along the back of the legs to the crotch. Now go to the other hind leg and do the same so the cuts join. Use your fingers to work the skin loose from the legs and belly up to the rib cage. If you use force you can pull the skin off the legs without cutting. Also work the skin loose from behind the tail with your fingers and work it up the back.

When the skin is all loose around the hind legs, belly and back, grasp the hind leg in one hand and the belly skin in the other and pull in opposite directions to peel the skin off like a glove towards the head. When you get to the front legs, grasp the leg skin in one hand and the leg in the other, turning the leg skin inside out and pull hard enough to separate the two without using the knife.

After the front legs are free, continue pulling on the skin until you get to the head. When the ears become visible as two small white bits of skin, cut them off at the base, and then pull the skin to the eyes and carefully cut around them. Strip the skin to the nose and mouth, cut off the nose from the inside and leave it on the skin.

After the 'rat skin is removed from the animal, it is placed on a stretcher to dry. Put it on the stretcher so the leg holes in the skin are on one side of the stretcher and the eye holes on the other. This makes sure that you have the back of the skin on one side of the stretcher and the belly on the other. Don't have half of the back or side on each side as is sometimes done by the amateur skinner. Pull the skin tight enough so it takes any loose folds of skin, but don't pull it overly tight. Tack the flap of skin at the base of the tail to the stretcher and the leg skin in the front to hold it in place. Leave it on the stretcher until it dries, which might take about three days. A dried muskrat skin feels about like paper, and will crackle like paper when it is handled.

Mink frequent about the same areas as muskrat, and it is expedient to trap them both at the same time. Mink travel on land much more than muskrats, and usually will travel the banks of rivers, lakes or ponds looking for their food, which consists of nearly any fish or animal that they can catch and subdue. Minnows, crayfish, mice and muskrats make up a large part of their diet.

A good mink set is the pocket set. Take a trapper's trowel or small shovel, a dyed #1-½ trap, some trappers wire, a small hand axe, and the front half of a muskrat carcass, consisting of the rib cage with the heart and lungs and liver intact. Find an area where mink tracks indicate that there are mink in the areas. Walk the banks of a creek at the waters edge. Try to imagine where a small animal like a mink would go if he were traveling the edge. Sooner or later you will find a place where vertical banks or a large rock or log will guide the mink into the water because it will be easier to enter the water than to continue along the edge. If the water is less than 1 foot deep, it will probably be a good place to make a set.

Near where the mink must enter the water, dig a horizontal hole right at the water line. Dig it straight back into the bank for at least a foot and then slant it upwards at least another 6 inches. Push the muskrat carcass into the hole to the very end so it is above the waterline. Now, at the entrance to this hole, set the trap, depress the pan so it will spring easily with the light touch of the mink. Stake the trap out in deep water so the trapped mink will quickly drown.

Check the traps about once a week. Most trappers check mink traps by wading up the stream or looking at it from some distance away so no human scent or disturbance is created around the trap, since it might make the mink shy away from the area.

When you catch the mink he will be wet and possibly muddy.

Wash the mud off as best you can at the trap site and possibly finish the job at home with a brush and water. Then dry the hair and skin him. Hang the mink up by one hind leg about chest high and make a knife slit through the foot pad and up the inside of the hind leg to the anus. Circle the anus and continue up the inside of the other hind leg till you get to the wire or clamp that is holding the opposite foot.

Use the fingers to pull the skin off the leg and foot pad. Use the tip of the knife to cut off the toes from the inside so the claws are retained on the skin. Skin out the base of the tail, pull the tail bone out and slit the tail skin up the center. Now change the wire over to the other foot and continue skinning out the left foot. Continue pulling the skin down over the mink's body by grasping the body in one hand and the skin in the other. Don't use the knife again until you get to the front feet which are cut off from the inside leaving the claws on the skin. Make the customary cuts at the eyes and nose. Be very carful not to nick the mink skin as it is very valuable and skinning cuts detract considerably from the price of the skin.

Stretch the mink skin on a mink stretcher. Male mink are much larger than female mink, and a different size stretcher is used for each. Remove any excess flesh on the skin, but don't attept to scrape the mink skin to flesh it. It is very thin.

Raccoon are another animal that is often easy to find by their bear-like paw prints. Coon are always hungry and will eat nearly anything. Therefore, they are usually trapped in bait sets.

Bait sets, or cubby sets, are made by first finding an area where raccoon are feeding. A cubby is made by arranging sticks, usually cut at the spot to form a frame about 8 inches wide, 10 inches high and a foot deep. The sticks are pushed in the ground to make the support and the back of the cubby is closed off, the front is left open. The sides and top of the cubby is covered over with branches or bark. Bait is placed in the cubby and a trap is set in front of it.

Raccoon are very strong animals, and it is expedient to use killer and connibear type traps for them. Usually the #220 trap is used, although in some states it has been outlawed.

Not because it isn't effective, because it is about the most effective trap on the market. The complaint has been that cats and dogs have been trapped accidently. However, in remote areas very few cats or dogs will fall into such a set, and usually they are legal.

An excellent bait for trapping raccoons is a muskrat carcass or a piece of beaver meat. If meat baits are not legal, or meat is hard to get for bait, use rotten fruits, syrup, honey or used cooking oil poured over grain. Place the bait in the back of the cubby.

The scent of the bait will attract the raccoon and he will investigate. When he finds he can't get in the back or sides of the cubby, he will try to enter the front which is the most open end. Then the trap will catch him. Other traps used for raccoon include all of the leg hold sizes from 1-½ and larger. If you use a leg hold trap for raccoon, be sure to stake it very well and use at least one or two swivels in the chain.

Raccoon are case skinned. That means like muskrats and mink they are skinned by making a single cut across the back of the hind legs. Then the skin is pulled off inside out. Do this by hanging the raccoon up by one hind leg with a wire placed around the heel. It should be hung at a comfortable height for working about chest high. The fur should be dry and combed clean of sticks and burrs before you start cutting. Now with a very sharp knife make a cut from the right hind leg to the heel to the crotch, circle the anus and reproductive organs and continue up the other side to the left heel. The hide is cut off above the feet. Next work the skin from the body at the base of the tail so you can get your finger clear around the tail bone at its base. Be very careful at this stage so you don't damage the tail skin, but grasp the tail bone in one hand and the tail skin in the other and pull it opposite directions to separate the two.

The tail skin should turn inside out as it is peeled back to the tip, leaving the tail bone attached to the body. If you can't pull it, cut the tail skin up the middle on the underside from the base about half way to the tip. Then pull it up this far and when this much is loosened, the rest should come easily. The raccoon has a large luxurious tail, and it should be carefully retained on the skin to receive top prices for the fur.

Then use both hands, pulling on the skin to work it inside out towards the head. When you get to the front legs the skin will stop. Use only your fingers, not the knife to work the front legs loose. When you get to the feet, circle cut from the inside to free the skin from the legs. Continue pulling it down to the head. The tip of the knife is used to cut the ears off at the base and free the eyes and the nose.

Some trappers roll the skinned hide up in a bag and put it in the freezer until the fur buyer comes around. Then they thaw it out so the buyer can examine it, and sell it green. However, some people won't have a freezer, especially in remote areas and must dry the skin so it will keep. Undried or unfrozen skins will quickly spoil. Fleshed dried skins also are worth more than frozen skins.

A raccoon skin has to be fleshed before it is placed on the stretcher to dry since it likely will have alot of fat adhering to it which will cause the skin to spoil. Raccoon skins are fleshed by placing them on fleshing beams or boards and using a fleshing knife or large dull butcher knife to scrape the fat away from the hide. Most of this fat is soft and will scrape away quite easily, but some is tough and must be sheared away. For this reason keep a sharp knife available. Often the meat around the head is hard to remove. Be sure not to cut the skin.

When the skin is well fleshed, it is placed on a raccoon stretcher and left to dry. A raccoon skin takes a long time to dry, but when it is done remove it from the stretcher and store in a cool dry place away from vermin and rodents until it is time to sell them.

The very thought of trapping beaver summons up images of mountain men and Hudson Bay trappers. Beavers are caught in either #330 connibear or #3 or #4 leg hold traps, or in snares. They live in colonies and most of the trapping is done in the winter after the ice locks the beaver into a small area.

Deep winter is the time when the pelts are prime. Fur animals "prime up" in winter, which means that their fur gets longer and thicker to protect them from the cold. Prime fur looks better and will last longer than unprime fur, so it is worth more money. Usually beaver trapping is regulated by an open and closed season set by the Department of Natural Resources in each state and province.

Most beaver are caught in either the bait set or the channel set in the winter when ice covers the pond.

Bait sets are made as follows: take a #330 body grip type trap. It should be dyed or painted black for maximum effectiveness. Also, you will need a supply of trappers wire and a hatchet or axe and an ice chisel. Holes can be chopped in the ice with an axe or sawed with a chain saw, but the ice chisel which is a round iron bar with a chisel blade welded to the bottom is much more useful for a beaver trapper than either the axe or chain saw.

Walk out on the ice of the pond to the beaver house. Near the house will be the beaver's feed bed. A feed bed is the tree branches and logs that the beaver stores for winter. The feed bed will look like a brush pile under the ice with the ends of the twigs sticking above the ice. At one edge of the feed bed, chisel a hole in the ice about 18 inches in diameter. The water under the hole should be at least 3 feet deep, but it must not be over 6 feet deep. Usually beaver ponds are between these depths. Now cut a dead pole 4 to 6 inches in diameter and about 10 feet long or about 4 feet longer than the depth of the water.

Sharpen one end of the pole and stick it down through the hole to the bottom of the pond and push it into the bottom a little ways. Now note the place on the pole that is just at the top of the ice and chop a little notch there to mark it. Pull the pole back up again. Now go find an aspen tree and cut off a bundle of the tenderest branches an inch in diameter or less. Leave the buds and twigs on but break the twigs into pieces about 1 foot long. Wire this bundle together and then wire it to the dead pole so when the pole is put back down it will be at least 1 foot under the lower surface of the ice. This means if the ice is 3 feet thick, you will put it about 4 feet under the notch you chopped on the pole. Wire it securely to the pole adjacent to or aligned with the pole.

Figure 4. Here my son and I inspect beaver traps. You have to "spud" a
hole in the ice to inspect the traps.

Now cock the #330 connibear and set it over the bait bundle so
one spring at the bottom. Wire the trap very well to the pole so
the trapped beaver doesn't get it loose.

Be very careful to not jar the trap and set it off, set the pole
up and push it back down through the hole in the ice and shove
it into the bottom so it is secure enough to stay in place without
bobbing back up or other wise moving. In an hour or so the
ice will freeze around the top of the pole again and hold it in
place. Also kick snow down in the ice hole to form a slush.
This will make it easier to chop the pole out again when you
want to look at the trap. Beaver traps are usually only looked

at once or twice a week since too much human activity can frighten the beaver into moving away from the area of the traps. Often you can look at the trap without pulling it up, by looking down through a hole chopped in the ice above the trap.

The channel set is made by first determining where the beaver swim through some narrow opening under the ice. Sometimes this will be a narrow channel that they have dug through an island or through boggy ground up to dry land. Sometimes these areas can be spotted in late winter, but usually trappers find them before the pond freezes over the snow falls. Then they can go out on the ice and chop through the ice in the right spot. Make the channel set by cocking and placing a #330 connibear type trap in the center of the channel where the water is 2 to 3 feet deep, or shallow enough so the beaver can't swim over the top of the trap. Stake the connibear in place by folding the spring back so a single pole can be pushed through the hole in both springs. Then place a slanting stick, called a dive stick, to keep the trap from swiveling around on the pole. This stick is placed through the inside of the jaws. Use dead sticks to stake off any part of the channel that the beaver can use to swim around the trap. Place the sticks about 3 inches apart. Drive them into the bottom so they are very secure.

If these two sets are made correctly and placed in good places, a trapper can expect to catch the beaver from a colony in a week or less. Be sure to pull your traps before catching all the beaver in a colony so they can reproduce and deliver a crop for the next year. If you can't do that, leave some colonies un-trapped so the surplus will spread from them to areas where there are no beaver.

That about completes the animals that can be trapped for a good supply of money in the southern regions of our coverage. In the north, the marten also will furnish a good supply of pelts.

Trap the marten by using baited cubbies like we covered for the raccoon or by making the running pole set. In this set, which will also take fisher and wolverine, a pole is leaned against the tree. The pole is 6 to 10 feet long. Bait, or an odor lure like skunk musk is placed at the top of the pole and the trap is set on the upper surface of the pole.

It is loosely wired in place so when the animal is caught it will fall free, the trap chain is securely anchored with nails or wire to the pole. Usually sticks are placed on each side of the pole to guide the animal over the trap. The 1½ trap is adequate for marten, but if fisher are apt to be caught also, use a #2 or #3 trap. If body grip traps are used, #220 connibears are adequate.

Fox and coyote usually can be counted upon to add some padding to the fur check, and are worth trapping, but only a few individuals ever get skilled enough to make important income trapping them. Both can be caught in the dirt hole set. The difference in setting for them is primarily the bait, size of traps used and placement of the traps.

The dirt hole set is made by digging a round hole in the ground about 4 inches in diameter and about 18 inches deep. It should be dug on about a 45 degree slant as animal burrows are dug. Dig it at the foot of a clump of grass, a clump of brush or under a rock so the animal can't approach from the upper side of the hole. Conceal the trap under the fresh dirt at the mouth of the hole. The trap must be covered with a large leaf or tissue paper or a piece of cloth. Then dirt is sifted over it so the dirt doesn't get under the pan and keep it from springing. If you wear scent-free gloves, you can pack the dirt around the jaws with your hands and eliminate the trap covering. But, be sure to leave a hollow under the pan.

The bait is placed at the bottom of the hole. Usually a small chunk of tainted meat is used for a bait. Muskrat meat, beaver meat or a dead mouse is often used.

When setting for fox, a #1½ or #1¾ foot grip trap is usually used. Coyotes are trapped in a #2 or larger foot grip trap. Usually body grip traps won't be successful in trapping the large predators since they are so wary.

In the far north, snares are also used for trapping wolves, coyotes and fox, as well as the small animals. Snares usually won't be as efficient as steel traps except by people skilled in their use.

Often raw furs can be home tanned also, and in many cases this increases their value considerably. Especially the least valuable like skunk, weasel and squirrel. These skins can be

Figure 5.   Her the authors son, Jim, Jr., skins a coyote. Proper care of
the animal's skin after it is caught is very important to receive
top wages.

tanned for a few cents in out-of-pocket expenses and sold for
$5.00 to $25.00, depending upon the market location and the use
for the skin.

Bobcat and lynx skins can be tanned for wall hangings, as can
fox and coyote and even timber wolves. Deer, elk and moose
hides also can be home tanned, either with the hair on or off.
Also, with a little home built equipment, the home tanner can do
custom tanning, This is well explained in my book **"The
Complete Book Of Tanning Skins and Furs",** Stackpole Books,
(1983).

Trapping certainly can add to the bush dwellers income, but there are many other ways to turn a buck in the woods.

In many areas of the country, there are certain herbs which are purchased by pharmaceutical companies to process into drugs used in medicines and industry. The most well known medicinal is ginseng, which now has reached a price of $275.00 a pound for the dried root. However, there are literally hundreds of other plants that are purchased regularly or occasionally by the drug trade. Usually they are sold by the collector to buyers who then package them in large quantities to sell to the drug companies. These buyers print a price list and directions for collecting and packaging the product. People who collect medicinal plants for sale are called wildcrafters.

A few of the valuable plants that are found in the states covered by this book are; ginseng, ginger, sasparilla, blackberry, milkweed, yellow lady slipper, strawberry, wintergreen, juniper, eastern white pine, balsam, poplar, black cherry, sumac, black willow, mullein and red clover. All of these plants and dozens of others are used from time to time by drug companies.

The pollen from various plant blooms are also used by drug companies to make preparations to test for pollen allergies. The pollens most in demand are ragweed, sages, sagebrush, elm, box elder, maple, ash, oak, cocklbur, pigweed and Russian thistle.

Pollen is collected in several different ways, but the basic method is to place a clean cloth under the blossom and tap it sharply so the pollen drops on the cloth. Usually pollen can be collected from the same plant for several days. However, when it turns dark it should not be collected.

Pollen collecting is most productive on a windless morning after the sun has dried the moisture from the plants. Pollen has to be air dried for about four days before being packaged, as it could mold if damp. When dry, it is strained through fresh nylon and packaged in clean screw top glass jars or in clean, dry, strong plastic bags.

Another occupation popular among people living in remote areas is guiding for big game and fishing. A top guide can command good wages, and is usually booked far in advance. In many states, including Alaska, guides are registered by the state, and have to pass an examination. In other states, such as Wisconsin, guides only have to be of good character. It is not unusual for a good guide to receive $100.00 per day for his services, and in some cases it is much higher. Once you learn the country around your remote area, you can offer your services.

Collecting, raising and selling fish baits is another enterprise that can be managed right along with guiding, trapping or several other ventures. Raising worms is, of course, a well known enterprise, and hundreds of farms are located all across the country, even up near Mount McKinley, Alaska. However, in the territory where fish are actually caught, all kinds of fish bait gets scarce at certain times of the year. Bait shops run out of night crawlers in midsummer and the price might go to $2.00 a dozen. In the spring when they are running, a good picker might collect 1,000 night crawlers each night for up to two weeks. Keep them in a refrigerator until midsummer and sell them. Of course, bait shops won't pay the full retail price, but if you can get 10 cents apiece for them, considerable profit can be realized.

Minnows are caught from the streams and lakes by trapping or seining. If you have a pond to use as a holding pond, seine out the minnows when they are abundant, as in early spring, and stock your pond. Then take orders from wholesalers or bait shops and deliver them.

Ice fishing in the northern states is a popular enterprise, and the demand for ice fishing baits are great. Mousies (horse fly larvae), meal worms (bot fly larvae), wax worms (bee moth larvae) and wigglers, which are the nymph stage of the may fly larvae are popular baits. Wigglers are gathered with wire mesh nets from the bottom of ponds that have many fly hatches, while the rest of the baits can be raised in a small area at home.

There are also several other products that can be collected from the wilds and sold to a ready market. Wild blackberries, wild blueberries and wild raspberries grow thickly enough in many areas to make picking them a profitable enterprise. They always find a ready market in grocery stores, or they can be sold from a roadside stand or they can be picked after taking orders from tourists or retail distributors.

In boggy areas in the north, spagnum moss grows. Spagnum

Figure 6.   Harvesting medicinal herbs for the drug trade can offer finan-
cial rewards. Here the author holds a ginseng plant. Ginseng
root currently sells for $197.00 a pound.

moss is the plant that peat moss is made of, and it is widely used
by nurseries for bedding plants, and it has several other uses.
Large moss marshes are cleaned of debris and are burned each
year to get rid of the grass. Moss is pulled with a rake that
looks like a hay fork with the tines bent at a 90 degree angle
to the handle. The moss is pulled up in wind rows and allowed
to partially dry. Then it is hauled out to be finished dried and
baled. In most areas, peat moss is trucked into large cities where
orders have already been placed. However, in many other
instances, or when you are just starting out, you might have
to build up your own markets.

Every year tree seed nurseries need seed from trees and wild shrubs for propgation. They purchase these seeds from collectors. White pine cones, spruce cones and red pine cones are purchases from collectors. Other seeds are; acorns, box elder, elm, wild cherry, maple and birch. The seeds have to be collected when they are at the right stage for picking so they will germinate. The state or province Department Of Natural Resources will be a good source of information on what seeds are needed and how to find a buyer, and how and when to collect the seeds.

There are a surprising number of occupations carried out in the back country also. In semi-rural areas there are postal clerks and rural mail carriers. School teachers are needed, as are school bus drivers and school janitors. Each rural county and township in the United States has a system of government, and county clerks, treasurers, forestors and social workers often have full time jobs.

In Alaska and Canada, as well as in the northwest states, fish canneries hire a considerable work force, and fishing boats also hire crews during the fishing season.

Chapter 4.
Tools For Backcountry Living

The reason man was able to rise above the lesser animals and control his environment was because he learned to make and use tools. Likely the first tool was a stone that he used for a hammer. With this simple device he was able to break sharp flakes from other rocks and create another tool, a cutting edge. With the cutting edge he could skin animals, fell and shape trees and make digging tools and gripping tools.

Modern day woodsmen also are going to need tools, and in fact, the success he will find in carving a life out of a remote area might depend on a great extent on how well he can use tools. Like ancient man, the tools the homesteaders will need can be roughly divided into pounding, cutting, gripping and digging tools. Pounding or hammering tools should include the claw hammer or carpenter's hammer, the mallet, the sledge or the splitting maul.

The carpenter's hammer is made up of a hammer head with a face for pounding nails, opposite a set of claws for pulling them. The handle is attached to the head through the eye. The handle is made of tough wood like hickory, or some are made from steel, usually covered with rubber or neoprene. If you purchase a wooden handled hammer, the handle will have to be replaced occasionally.

Some carpenters prefer the wooden handled hammers because of the "spring action" that only wood imparts to the hand when driving nails. Replacement wooden handles can be purchased or they can be made by the cabineer if he has a tough straight grained piece of wood to work with. The expedient settler will probably have a good straight grained piece of trunk wood stored in the woodshed or under the cabin eave where it will season slowly to make handles from.

Even with "store bought" handles, the end to be inserted into the eye of the hammer has to be reshaped. This is usually started with a wood or knife rasp and finished with sandpaper or a piece of glass to make it smooth, keep trying the handle to see if it fits in the eye of the hammer head until you tap the handle into the eye of the hammer head to the proper depth. Usually this is done by pushing the head on the handle as far as possible and then striking the opposite end of the handle vertically on a solid but flexible surface, like a wooden block. Inertia then will jam the handle into the head.

Once the head has slid into the handle to the proper posititon, it should be checked for "plum", that is, it should be perpendicular to the head. Next, wedges are driven into the upper end of the head to make it super tight. Purchased hammer handles usually have wedges as part of the packages, but if you make your handle you can make new wedges or reuse the ones from the old handle.

The other hammers useful to the settler, the sledge, splitting maul and mallet also are rehandled in the same way.

The beginning builder often has trouble driving a nail without bending it. This can be corrected by holding the hammer at about the same level as the nail head, keep your eye on the nail head throughout the hammer stroke so the hammer face strikes it squarely.

The claws on a carpenter's hammer, of course, are put there like the eraser on a pencil to correct mistakes. If a nail is too hard to pull, place a wooden block under the hammer head to increase the leverage.

Sledges are used for driving posts or stakes, breaking rocks, moving building logs into proper alignment or a multitude of other chores where a heavy blow is required. Mallets are used for driving wood chisels and gouges. If you are going to do mechanical repairs, work with rivets, cold chisels or form sheet metal, a ball peen hammer is needed. This hammer is familiar to most people since it looks like a claw hammer except that it has a round, peening surface on the back of the head where the claws of a claw hammer are located.

Axes are, of course, what nearly everyone thinks of when they imagine a life in the backwoods. There are two general types, the double bit and the single bit. The double bit axe is the choice of some loggers and cabin builders because one blade can be kept super sharp for notching and cutting limbs and the other blade can be used for rougher work.

A very good axe for the cabineer is a single blade axe with a four pound head and a (standard) 3 foot handle. The blade can be kept sharp for chopping and the back or blunt edge of the axe can be used as a maul or even for fighting off hungry brown bear.

Axes are sharpened with a file and finished with a sharpening stone. For chopping, the blade should be tapered gradually to a fine edge from about 1½ inches back. For splitting, the edge is sharpened to a chisel point.

Axes are very dangerous. The author spent time in the hospital when an overhanging limb deflected the axe blade enough so that it drove into my foot instead of into the log I was chopping. I was unable to work for about four months, spent considerable time in the hospital and will always be partially crippled, so I know whereof I speak. Deep in the wilderness, avoid their use as much as possible. If you use them, be sure the area all around you is clear of overhanging limbs, clothes lines and such obstructions that can catch the axe on the downward swing and deflect it. Always chop on the side of the log away from your feet, and don't try to split wood just lying flat on the ground.

Be sure the axe head is kept tight so it doesn't fly off and hit someone, and be sure to replace the handle when it gets cracked or frayed. Further, don't pound on metal or rocks with the back of the axe because it is going to get up stresses in the metal that will almost certainly cause it to break sooner or later.

Far and away the most important tool for the woods dweller is the saw. Hand saws are the safest to use and therefore a good choice for use on remote sites where medical help would be hard to find. With the proper saw you can cut down a huge tree, cut up meat, or saw metal, and of course, you can build a cabin.

A very good hand saw for cutting down trees and sawing them into pieces is the bow saw. Sometimes called the "Swede saw", this device consists of a bow shaped frame that supports a coarse toothed saw blade. With this saw, one man can cut down an 8 inch tree in 30 seconds. However, it does require experience to use properly. Bow saws come in a variety of sizes, with the larger saw, of course, being used for the largest trees.

The chain saw is used by most modern day woodsmen to cut firewood, clear land and make cabins. With a chain saw, one man can do the work of two or three working with hand sawes. They are also very versatile. A chain saw can be used to make a saddle notch in a log, saw out boards for shelves or the roof, carve furniture out of large logs and nearly everything else that saws are used for. In good timber, one man can cut down and saw into proper lengths all the logs needed for a cabin in one or two days.

The disadvantages of chain saws is that they need gasoline and oil, they are noisy, can start fires, need expensive repairs from time to time, are heavy to transport, and a good one is expensive. They also are dangerous to use.

Nevertheless, most people will definitely want a chain saw to work with. But, the beginner should become fimiliar with the large assortment of saws so he or she can make a proper choice when you buy one for back of beyond. The two most important parts of a chain saw are the blade size and the engine size. The blade must be long enough to cut through large trees, but not so long it is unwieldly. An 18 inch blade can be used to cut a 30 inch tree by sawing from both sides and therefore will be long enough for almost all uses. No need to get a longer blade, but a shorter one might not be satisfactory for some usage.

Chain saws are manufactured with different size engines. Most start with 2 cubic inch engines and increase in size to 5 cubic inch engines, and some professional saws used by loggers in extremely big timber are even larger. A chain saw with a 2 cubic inch engine would only be useful for light duty cutting, such as limbing a tree or cutting brush or small trees. The chain saw that combines light weight with the most power will have at least a 3 cubic inch engine. I have used a well known model with a 3.7 cubic inch engine for several years to build log buildings and cut my firewood. It does a competent job. Be sure to get a saw made by a well known company so you can get spare parts for it without undue trouble.

Before taking to the woods, the settler should become familiar with his saw. He should know how to mix the gasoline and oil and have the containers to do it with. He should know how to sharpen the teeth on the chain, how to disassemble the chain and bar and clean the sprocket. He should know where the air filter and gas filter are located so they can be cleaned, and how to change the spark plug. Also, how to replace a broken starter rope. He should become as familiar as possible with complete disassemble and inspection of the saw for major repairs if they become necessary.

Each new saw will have a manual with it which instructs the new owner in maintenance and sharpening, but in case you buy a used saw or lose your manual, the following information might be important.

The saw chain will need more attention then any part of your saw. It will probably become loose after you saw awhile and must be tightened. It will also get dull and must be sharpened. The best way to tell if your chain saw needs sharpening is to watch the wood chips or sawdust it makes. A properly sharpened saw shaves off large chips, after it dulls it will cut smaller chips. With experience you can tell by the speed of the cut also if it needs sharpening. Generally the chain will need sharpening after every third or fourth refueling. But, if you dig the saw into dirt or hit a stone, the chain will probably need immediate sharpening.

Chains are sharpened with a round file. Usually sharpening guide and file is included with the saw. Be sure to check for these items before you go back of beyond. Saw files are low cost items and it is well to take at least four along. I put a wooden handle on mine and paint the wood orange so it doesn't get lost.

To sharpen the chain, stop the engine, place the saw on a flat surface such as a stump and put on a pair of gloves. The chain will have to be loose enough to be pulled around the bar by hand. If it can't, it is too tight or the drive sprocket or grove in the bar is filled with sawdust or debris. This should be corrected before the saw is started again.

Use the sharpening guide, or if you don't have a guide, study the angle on the teeth and be sure you maintain this angle as you sharpen the saw. It will only require a few light strokes to sharpen each tooth. Sharpen one side, turn the saw around and sharpen the other. From time to time the depth guage or rakers have to be filed down so the cutting edge of the teeth can engage the wood.

Saw chains can get broken if they get too loose, get caught in a cut or get badly worn. You will need to take replacement teeth and links along with you. It is also expedient to take an entire replacement chain, so not much time need be lost if a chain breaks it can be repaired at your leisure.

About all it takes to fix a broken chain is replacement parts, a flat file, a hammer and small punch or nail for driving the rivets. Usually the cutters aren't replaced, especially in a worn chain. They are just left out and new tie bars are put in. This won't noticeably affect the cutting performance of the chain. Remove the broken links by filing off the heads of the rivets. Drive them out, put in new parts and peen the heads of the rivets. Be sure not to flatten the end of the rivets so much that they restrict the swivel action of the chain.

After the cutting is done for the day, the saw chain should be removed and placed in a container of light oil. This will greatly increase the life and performance of the chain. Most chain saw oiling systems are only marginally effective, and even during the days work, oil should be dripped on the blade to supplement the oiling system.

Although anytime the chain saw is running, it is capable of injuring the user or a bystander, probably the most hazardous part of woodcutting is falling the tree. When you are doing this you are in a risk situation from both the running chain saw and the falling tree. Generally speaking, you should not cut trees if the wind speed is high and swirling. You should also never cut a tree if it has loose hanging limbs that cannot be removed, or if you have to change the direction of the trees natural fall, or if you have no way to move away from the tree as it is falling. Partially rotten trees also are hazardous.

The following illustrates good chain saw, tree falling techniques and should be thoroughly studied. The information has been taken from the Sears Chain Saw Manual with permission.

OPERATION
Starting
1. Move chain saw at least 10 feet away from fueling point.
2. Take proper starting position with saw on the ground (in a debris-free area) right toe in rear handle and left hand on front handle (Figure 7).
3. Set your choke and pull the starter handle slowly until a slight resistance is felt (between 2 and 4 inches) then finish the pull sharply.
4. When saw coughs, push choke half way in to prevent engine "flooding".
5. The saw should be set at idle and the chain should not move.

Check before you cut.
1. Check the chain tension.
2. Check to see if the chain and bar are getting enough oil. Throttle up to cutting speed for a few seconds, holding bar nose approximately six inches from test surface. Enough oil should be thrown from chain to mark test surface (Figure 8). Do not allow bar nose to touch test surface.

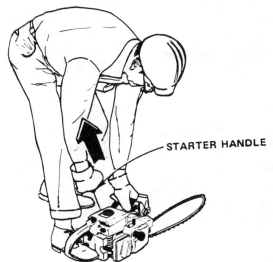

STARTER HANDLE

Figure 7.

6"

BAR NOSE

Figure 8.

Using good sawing technique

1. Practice cutting a few limbs or small logs to get the "feel" of your saw.

2. Use a firm grip (thumbs opposing fingers) with left hand on front handle and right hand on rear handle. Keep a secure balanced footing to the left of the saw and don't over reach (Figure 9).

3. Squeeze throttle lever fully before starting the chain into wood. The chain will cut more efficiently with engine at top speed.

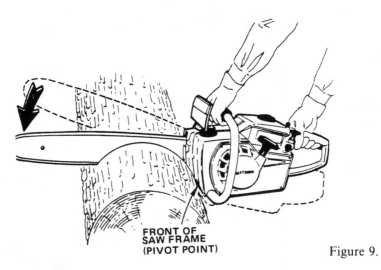

FRONT OF
SAW FRAME
(PIVOT POINT)   Figure 9.

4. Start cutting with the front of Saw Frame against the log or tree and pivot as you cut so that the Bar Nose enters the cut last (Figure 9).

5. Allow the chain to cut for you and hold saw so that the chain runs free in the opening cut. You need not rock the saw back and forth in the cut or use great force to cut; in fact using excessive force can result in bar, chain, or engine damage.

6. Keep saw chain at cutting speed until bar is completely free of cut, then release throttle lever to idle engine while planning the next cut.

Good Tree Falling Technique
SIZE UP THE TREE.
1. Determine natural falling direction . . .
   a. toward the direction of natural lean.
   b. toward the side with more or heavier branches.
   c. (if heavily leaved) with the direction of the wind.
2. Avoid falling a tree . . .
   a. if it shows signs of rot which may make falling unpredictable.
   b. if it's natural falling direction must be changed to avoid obstacles.
   c. if hanging dead limbs ("window makers") cannot be removed before falling.
   d. if wind is strong or gusty.

DIRECTION
OF FALL

Figure 10.

PLAN YOUR ESCAPE ROUTE. Choose a route back and to one side of the direction of tree fall (Figure 10). You should plan a route that will place you at least twenty feet from the stump at the time the tree hits the ground.

CLEAR THE BRUSH AND DEBRIS from around the tree and along your escape route. Examine tree in cutting area and remove dirt or foreign material which might dull or break the chain as you cut.

FALL THE TREE.
1. Under cut ("notch") the tree on the side of natural fall (Figure 11).
   a. Make the first cut horizontally 1/3 the tree diameter at a comfortable working height.
   b. Finish the undercut with a sloping cut to meet but not cross the first.
   c. Clean out the undercut wood.
2. Backcut ("falling cut") the tree opposite the notch (Figure 11).
   a. Make the horizontal falling cut opposite the side of natural fall, at least 2 inches above the horizontal undercut.
   b. For trees larger than bar length make two falling cuts pivoting bar nose in last, in on one side, then pivoting in from the other to complete the cut. (Figure 12).
   c. Some trees may need to be pushed into the undercut. Drive wedges into the backcut, stopping often to drive wedges tight but taking care not to place them where they will interfere with cutting or direction of fall. Use plastic or wood wedges so that they cannot dull saw chain if accidentally hit.
   d. DO NOT CUT COMPLETELY THROUGH TO THE UNDERCUT. Leave at least a 2 inch hinge to hold and guide the tree down in the direction you planned and keep the tree from snapping off the stump. Make sure to keep the hinge a uniform thickness to prevent the tree from pivoting on the stump.

ESCAPE. As your backcut nears the undercut, watch the tree top and the cut for signs of movement. Be alert — as soon as the tree starts to move, pull your saw from the tree, turn it off, put it down, and move away quickly on your escape route. If your saw is pinched in the backcut — Don't wait until the falling tree frees it. Shut it off and leave it! Be alert to conditions which might alter your planned escape route and watch where you are going!

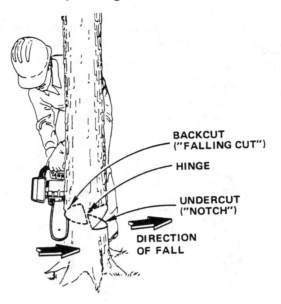

Figure 11.

Figure 12.

STUDY THE STUMP. Improve your falling technique by analyzing your work (Figure 13).

1. Did the undercuts meet without crossing?
2. Was the backcut horizontal, parallel to the undercut and at least 2 inches above it?
3. Was the hinge at least 2 inches thick and of uniform thickness?

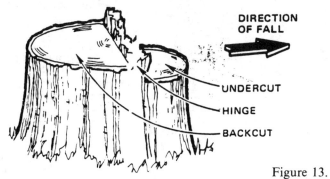

DIRECTION OF FALL

UNDERCUT

HINGE

BACKCUT

Figure 13.

Good tree falling technique

PREVENT KICKBACK. Never let the moving chain at the bar nose catch or stub itself or the bar will recoil back and up (Figure 14).

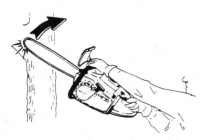

Figure 14.

CUTTING SMALL BRUSH. Use extreme care when cutting small size brush and saplings because slender material may catch the saw chain and be whipped toward you or pull you off balance.

PINCHED SAW. If your saw should become pinched in a cut, stop the engine before removing it.

Limbing

1. Cut branches and limbs from the felled tree starting at the base, working towards the top. Leave the larger lower limb to support the tree as you work.
2. Extreme care should be taken cutting limbs which may spring out in any direction.
3. As often as practical when limbing, stand on opposite side of trunk from limbs you are cutting off.
4. Large lower branches which support the felled tree's weight should first be top cut, then under cut so that the cut opens away from the saw, not closing on and pinching it (Figure 15).

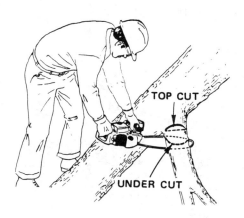

Figure 15.

Bucking (cutting logs)

1. Stand to side of the saw, not behind it and take a position uphill of possible log roll.
2. Logs resting on the ground for their entire length can be bucked from the top ("overbuck"). Stop cutting before passing through the log; it takes only a few seconds of cutting dirt to ruin a chain. Roll log over to finish.
3. After completing a cut, wait for the saw chain to stop before you move the chain saw.

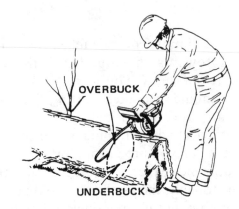

Figure 16.

4. Logs that are only supported on one end can be cut from below from 1/3 log diameter ("underbuck") then finished from the top (Figure 16).

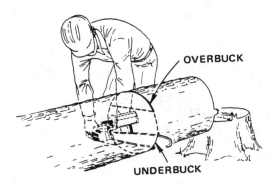

Figure 17.

5. Logs that are only supported on both ends can be over-bucked 1/3 log diameter then finished from the bottom (Figure 17).
6. Use soft wedges (wood or plastic) if necessary to prevent it from pinching saw bar in the cut.
7. Smaller, lighter logs may need to be blocked to prevent them from rolling off their supports.
8. Always stop the engine before moving from tree to tree.

Pruning (cutting limbs from standing trees)

1. Do not saw on ladders, platforms in trees or in any other position which might endanger your balance and thus cause loss of positive saw control.

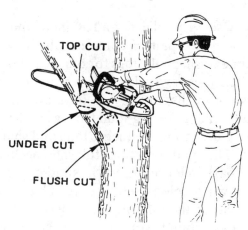

TOP CUT

UNDER CUT

FLUSH CUT

Figure 18.

2. When removing a limb from a growing tree, make an undercut ¼ limb diameter near the trunk and finish with a tip cut a little farther out from the trunk. After removing the limb, flush cut the stub near the trunk (Figure 18).

No one can develop a cabin site without digging equipment. You will need a few shovels and other digging tools to level the ground, shape foundation excavations, make a garden and even dig worms for fishing. A minimum tool compliment would be at least one well made, long handled shovel. However, you can also make use of a short handled shovel, a large scoop shovel, a tiling shape, a post hole digger, a pick, a grub hoe, a garden hoe and possibly a hand cultivator if you are going to have a garden.

Digging tools require little care other then keeping them rust free, replacing the handles and sharpening the cutting edges. Next in importance to digging tools might be a portable hand winch or come-a-long. They are almost indespensible for lifting heavy logs into place when you are building your cabin. They also can be used for moving fallen trees off the trail, hanging by game animals for skinning, freeing a stuck snowmobile or truck or dozens of other uses where a man's strength is not equal to the task at hand. A portable jack will also be used again and again, especially when you are building.

You will also need a set of mechanics tools that contain at least one set of combination open end and box end wrenches, screw drivers, a pair of vise grip pliers, and 8 inch and 12 inch adjustable wrench, and two pair of common pliers.

When it comes time to shape the logs for building, you can use a large wooden mallet, a set of wood chisels, a brace and bit and a set of extra long wood drills, unless you have access to wood auguers. You can make a log peeling spud from a small section of automobile springs. Cut it about 12 inches long and sharpen one end to a chisel edge. The spud is most useful when peeling logs in the spring when the bark in loose. Insert the spud under the strip of bark and lift up. It will tear loose a long strip of bark and make peeling a log much easier then if you use an axe.

For moving the logs around, you can use a picaroon, a cant hook and a set of lug hooks. Lug hooks look like a huge pair of ice tongs and they are used to pick up logs by two men. They are especially useful when logs have to be transported short distances, since two men can pick up one end of the log and work together to drag it. A picaroon resembles a short handled axe but has a spike instead of a blade. The spike is driven into the ends of logs they can be moved or dragged without having to handle them. Some picaroons have an axe blade on one side for trimming off limbs and projections on the log when they are being sorted. A cant hook has a long wooden handle on a spike and hook device, and is used for rolling logs.

It is also useful to have a pair of log snubbers for holding a pair of logs in a certain portion for making the notch and for several other uses. They can be made by any metal working shop, or at home. Simply cut ⅝ inch reinforcing rod into 2 foot lengths, sharpen each end, heat and bend 3 inches of each end to a 90 degree angle.

Wood planes are needed also if you intend to do finish work. They are used especially for planing doors, around windows and for several other applications where small amounts of material must be removed. A jack plane is used for cutting with the grain of the wood, and a block plane for cutting across it. Nail sets, linoleum knives and a wing divider also are needed. A wing divider is used to project the notch outline on succeeding layers of logs. It is shaped like a compass used for making circles on paper. The 12 inch divider is the size that I use. A divider can be obtained from sheet metal shop suppliers or from carpenter supply businesses.

Every building has to have a foundation, and unless you use the Alaskan method of sinking a series of wooden posts and building on them, you will be working with concrete or stone. For working concrete you need a mortor trowel, a mortor box, a float and hoe or shovel for mixing concrete. For stone work you need a stone chisel, star drill, and a five pound mallet for driving the drill and chisel.

Don't forget files and stones for sharpening your knives, axes and other tools. The tool chest should contain at least one small three cornered file for sharpening hand saws, one medium three cornered file, plus one medium and one large flat file. Make handles for your files by peeling a section of tree branch about 1 inch in diameter and 4 inches long. Drive this onto the tang of the file. Paint it a bright color and save alot of time looking for the file if you lay it down outside.

Suggested Tools For The Cabineer
Carpenters hammer
Ball peen hammer
4 pound sledge
Single blade axe
Pick
Bow saw
Chain saw and accouterments
Long handled hand shovel
Short handled shovel or tiling spade
Gardening hoe
Hand winch
A set of mechanics tools
100 feet of ⅝ rope
two 25 foot log chains, equipped with hooks
Snowmobile
Farm tractor equipped with front end loader
Rubber tired wheel barrow

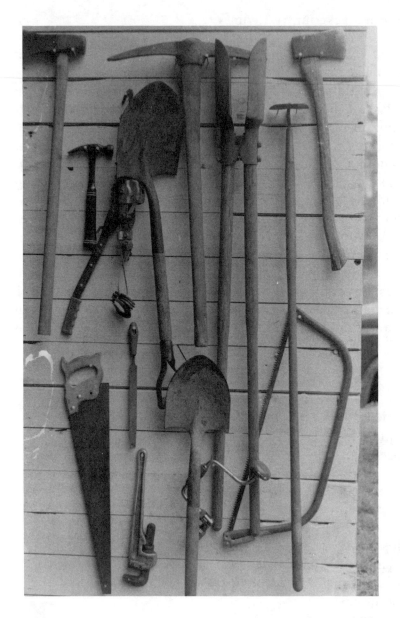

Figure 19.

Tools And How To Use Them

Using the tools on this board, the cabineer can carve a homestead from the wilderness. From left to right on top row:

A.   Sledge. Use this for driving stakes, breaking rocks and other uses where a smaller hammer won't do the job.

B.   Carpenters hammer

C.   Cable hoist often called a "come-a-long".

D.   Pick. For digging roots and breaking up hard ground so it can be removed.

E.   Post hole digger

F.   Garden hoe

G.   Single blade axe

Bottom Row:

H.   Hand saw. Although power saws are usually used now-a-days, don't forget that only a few decades past, this tool was used to build beautiful elaborate houses and you can build your cabin with one.

I.   Long handled shovel

J.   Brace and bit. Used for drilling holes in logs and boards where no electricity is available to power an electric drill.

K.   Bow saw. A bow saw can be used to cut down trees for building a log cabin or for cutting firewood. A properly sharpened bow saw in the hands of an experienced sawyer will cut trees very fast.

Figure 20.   Trappers often build small "line" cabins and live in them while they are trapping remote areas.

Chapter 5
Building The Log Cabin

I have never talked to a person that yearned to get back to nature that didn't think a log cabin was the best dwelling for living in the woods. It is a fine structure when it is made right, and will probably continue to dominate the backcountry, as it should.

The first step in building a log cabin is to find a suitable site. This statement isn't as redundant as it sounds. You can hardly build a log cabin on the top of a high cliff, and you wouldn't build in the middle of a swamp, or where avalanches or loose rocks come tumbling down the mountain on a regular basis. Use great care in selecting the site. See the section on the portable cabin for more information on this. Moreover, you can't build a log cabin where there are no logs, unless they can be brought in by water or road.

However, it is possible to transport logs in a number of different ways. If horses can be brought in to the site, they are ideal for skidding logs, because they can pull the logs through forests and over rough ground. In winter, a heavy duty snowmobile can pull a good size log. Before pulling the log, make a packed trail by running the snowmobile back and forth several times in the same track. Then let it freeze overnight for two or three nights and pack it down again by running the snowmobile on it. When it freezes again it will hold up almost any size log.

Chain the log to the snowmobile trailer hitch. Be sure the forward edge of the log is slanted so it doesn't gouge into the trail. It usually works best to tow the log by the butt since the forward motion lifts the log somewhat, which makes it slide easier. If you know beforehand that you will be skidding logs with a snowmobile, have a sheet metal shop build a skidding "leader" for you. This is merely a heavy duty sheet of metal that is slipped under the log to form a runner that will slide easily. A leader will remove at least half of the friction that is generated from sliding a log.

If you will build along a lakeshore or river, logs can be floated into the site. We have pulled 25 foot logs behind our boat which is powered by a 5 horsepower motor. The worst problem associated with floating logs is moving them from where they fall, into water that is deep enough to float them, then taking them out of the water again. Usually this is done with a come-along type cable winch. A cable winch also can be used to move logs short distances, as when they are cut near to the building site. This device is also used to move logs up to the proper place in the building after the walls get too high to lift them by hand.

However, in many areas covered by this book, it will be possible to use a tractor with a front end loader to skid the logs into position and lift them into place as they are fitted. In my opinion, this almost is the ideal device to have when building a log cabin. It uses are almost unlimited when taming the backcountry.

All logs should be cut and peeled about 6 months before the cabin is built. They should be dried as much as possible during this time, by placing them on short sections of scrap logs to keep them off the ground. In high precipitation areas, they should also be covered with a roof of tar paper or similiar material so the air can circulate around them, but yet be protected from the rain.

Figure 21.   If you can arrange to take a tractor with a front end loader with you when you take to the woods, your work will be made immensely easier.

Logs peel the easiest in the spring when the sap is running, and if possible peel the logs one spring and let them dry until time to start building the next spring. They can be peeled almost anytime, but when the bark is frozen it is more difficult to remove. Use an axe or drawknife to peel the logs.

Most log cabins are built from spruce in the far north because it is the most readily available log that is large enough and symetrical enough to make good log building material. Most any tree, if it is large enough, can be used for cabin building material. The author built a log cabin from large aspen trees, and they were perfectly satisfactory except for a tendency to crack.

Except in the far north, all logs but cedar, should be treated with some type of preservative. The most economical, being the material called black top sealer. Blacktop sealer is mineral oil and will keep any cabin from rotting. Many commercial materials are also available for treating cabin logs. Do not use creosote, as it can cause noxious odors and fumes. In the dry climate of the far north, many cabin logs are not treated, but left in the natural state with good results.

The 20' x 20' Alaskan log cabin outlined in this book require twenty-eight 12" x 25' logs for the side walls. However, if logs are scarce, you can use short lengths on each side of the windows and doors. Eleven 4 inch diameter logs for floor joists, six 6" x 25' logs for roof purlins, twenty-two 12 foot 4 inch diameter poles for rafters. This amount of logs can be cut in a day or two by one man equipped with a good chain saw, especially if the logs are near to each other.

While these logs are drying, you can build the foundation. A log foundation is adequate for most areas. Use the largest diameter logs available, dig the holes down to bedrock or solid mineral soil, if possible. In some areas this will require a hole for each log footing to be 6 foot deep, but in most cases 2 to 4 feet deep will be adequate. The logs used for footings should be treated with three coats of a good preservative. Set them in the holes so the ends project about 12 inches above the ground.

The tops of footing logs might have to be cut after they are set to make them level with each other. Use a carpenter's level or string level to mark them. Use a log miter box as a guide in cutting the logs so they are "square" and level. Be sure the foundation is square and straight by using the suggestions outlined in the portable cabin section.

After the footings are in place, the first two logs are fitted to the footings and spiked in place. A flat area has to be hewed on the under surface of the first two logs so they will set level on the footings. Use 8 inch spikes for fastening the first logs to the footings. Set them in holes drilled in the logs if necessary.

The first two logs are also notched for the floor joists. The joists are place on 2 foot centers. The floor joists are set in notches 3 inches deep. The upper surface of the floor joists are hewed so they have a flat surface for installing the flooring. The floor joists are spiked to the logs. Use 20d spikes.

Next, the wall logs can be notched and fitted into place. Use the largest logs on the bottom rows because they will stabilize the upper logs. All the logs are fitted the same way. First, lift it into position so it is laying on the bottom logs. Roll it around until the straightest, flattest surface is down. Mark that surface with chalk and roll the log over so the chalk mark is up. Then use a chain saw or sharp axe to hew a straight flat surface on the log. This hewn area should be about 3 inches wide. Now roll the log over again until it is located atop the logs it will rest on in the exact position that it will reside in the wall.

The next step is to mark for the notch. The tool to use for this task is a wing divider. A divider looks like a large compass. With the divider held vertically, measure the radius of the log that is supporting the log you are working with. This will represent the depth of the notch. Lock the divider at this measurement so the legs won't move. Now, again with the divider held vertically, place the lower leg of the divider on the bottom log, scribe its upper surface on the log tobe notched by moving the divider in an arc over the radius of the lower log. (See figure 22) Be sure to push the point of the upper leg against the upper log with enough force so it makes a legible scratch mark. When this is

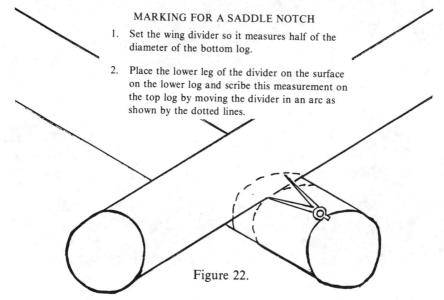

MARKING FOR A SADDLE NOTCH

1. Set the wing divider so it measures half of the diameter of the bottom log.

2. Place the lower leg of the divider on the surface on the lower log and scribe this measurement on the top log by moving the divider in an arc as shown by the dotted lines.

Figure 22.

done, leave the divider set as it is and move over to the opposite side of the log and scribe it in the same way. This marks both surfaces of the logs to be notched.

Darken these marks with chalk or heavy pencil so they are easy to see, and use the chain saw to cut out the material to form the notch. This type of notch is called a saddle notch. The notch should be made as perfectly formed as possible. However, this is easier than it looks, and if the prospective builder will practice a little on scrap materials before attempting the cabin building, it should pose little difficulty.

Figure 23.   Make the saddle notch by sawing several cuts from the top surface down to the mark. Chip out the material between the cuts with the axe.

When laying up the logs, be sure to alternate the butts so the wall will stay as level as possible. Also, use the same size logs for a complete round, if possible. It is very difficult to fit different size logs in to each other. Considerable time can be saved by laying out similar logs before the building starts so each round will have logs of like diameter.

After each round is completed, it should be pinned to the round underneath. The pinning is done at each end and wherever the logs are cut for a door or window. This prevents the logs from "bulging" out of position. The logs are pinned together with 12 inch spikes. First, each pinning point is marked at the center of the log, 12 inches from the notch at the ends and 6 inches from the ends of the logs where doors and windows are installed. Then a ⅜ inch diameter hole is drilled completely through the top log, but it need not enter the bottom log. Follow the ⅜ inch hole with a ¾ inch hole to about half the diameter of the log. Now drop a 12 inch spike down in the hole and drive it into the bottom log. A five pound hammer is a good tool for driving these big spikes. When the surface of the log is reached, use a punch to drive the spike. It must set well below the upper surface of the top log.

Concrete reinforcing rod or wooden dowles are also used for pinning logs together. The procedure is substantially the same.

Continue building up the logs a round at a time until the walls are about 6 feet high. Measure for the windows and doors so the walls can be pinned as they go up.

FOOTING, BOTTOM LOG AND FLOOR JOISTS

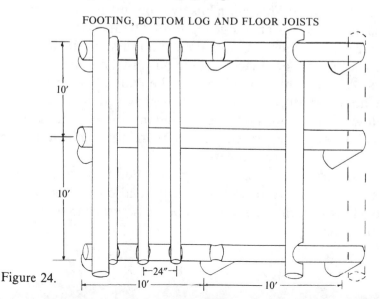

Figure 24.

Lay a strip of 6 inch thick fiberglass insulation on the log underneath before pinning each log in place. If the logs fit good, that should be all the chinking needed. Keep the walls vertical on the inside by using a carpenter's level to check each one before it is pinned.

The next step is to cut out the openings for the windows and doors. There are many methods of doing this, but the way I like is to spike a 2 x 8 plank on each side of the openings so the inner edge of the plank can be used for a guide for sawing. This plank also holds the logs in place as they are cut.

Remember to cut the window and door opening wide enough so a 2 x 10 or 2 x 12 board can be used for a frame. This will require an opening 3½ inches wider then the window sash or door frame. Be sure to measure carefully before you cut through these logs. The ends of the logs are held in place with the board frame. This frame is nailed to the logs but holes for the nails should be drilled through the frame. These holes should be slotted so the logs can settle downward as the cabin dries.

When all the wall logs are in place, the gable logs can be installed. The gable logs are not notched, but flattened on two sides, placed on top of each other and spiked in place. This structure has a 3 foot rise in the center. The gable logs are notched for the roof purlins after they are spiked in place, or if desired, the purlins can be put in place and the gable logs notched to fit: This should be done carefully so a minimum of chinking is needed. This cabin has two roof purlins on each side besides the ridge log. The ridge log should be at least 10 inches in diameter since it must support the roof and snow load.

The roof rafters are placed on the purlins. They are on 2 foot centers. A rafter must be placed at the ends of the purlins to create an overhang. The roof can be covered with plywood sheathing and composition, or wooden shingles. If hauling plywood to the site presents a problem, then milled 1 inch lumber can be used for roof sheathing.

The traditional way of building the roof was to place the rafters side by side to form a solid roof and cover it with sod. This is alot of extra work but will be satisfactory in low precipitation areas.

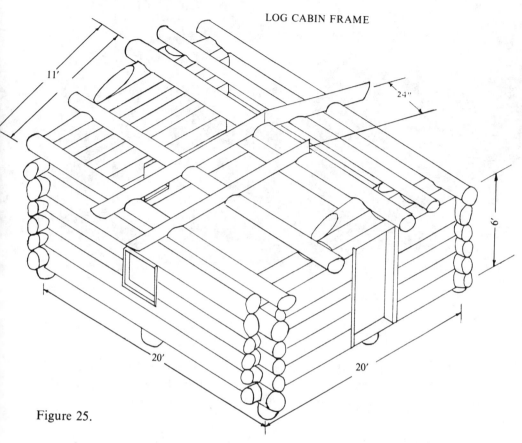

LOG CABIN FRAME

Figure 25.

For a really warm cabin, staple 12 inch thick fiberglass insulation to the roof boards between the rafters. The more you can insulate your cabin, the less time you have to spend cutting wood. You can go fishing instead. If you want to put in a ceiling, of course, this will also help the cabin to stay warm.

There is nothing wrong with using factory built prehung doors and windows if you can get them to the site. They save time and result in a better and more weather tight fit, in most cases. However, most are designed for frame buildings with milled siding so you may have to special order them if you want a rustic trim. Non-prehung doors and windows are set inside milled lumber frames. The window sashes are bracketed between 1 x 4 planed lumber. The door frame is made with planed 2 x 10 lumber. The door is hung inside this frame. The door is sealed

Figure 26.   I built this log cabin working in the winter. Note that the roofing paper is put on as fast as the roof sheathing is applied. This
prevents moisture from debilitating the roof boards.

with 1 x 3 planed lumber or even conventional door stop. Again,
be sure you are certain of the size of the rough opening before
you cut the logs.

The floor can be made of most conventional flooring material
with good results. Probably the flooring that will match the
scheme of the log cabin, the best is tongue and groove hardwood
flooring. However, ½ inch exterior grade plywood put down in
two opposing layers is perfectly satisfactory, as are many other
materials. Be sure to get a tight fit between the flooring and the
side walls. Seal any cracks in the floor to keep out drafts.

If you have the time and patience, you can make a hewn floor
by hewing three flat sides on logs and installing them over the
floor joists. This reportedly took up most of one winter for hardy
pioneers who settled the land. In the interval between moving in

and getting the floor done, they used a dirt floor. Hewn flooring can be produced much quicker in modern times with a chain saw and chain saw lumber mill.

Regardless of the material used, some type of insulation should be installed under the flooring. The cabin exterior should be sealed between the bottom log and the ground so drafts don't blow under the structure.

A wood stove will be a dominant part of the floor plan. Study the floor plan illustration for a way to place the household amenities and still have some room to move around. An excellent wood stove chimney can be formed with metal striple wall chimney made for that purpose. The chimney and roof must be sealed with flashing. In most cases, the flashing is included as part of the metal chimney package.

Excellent wood stoves are available and a small airtight heater will keep this cabin warm in nearly any weather. If a wood cook stove is also used, it should have its own chimney. If you don't care to cook on a wood stove, L.P. gas or gasoline stoves can be used to supplement cooking done on the top of the wood heater.

If you are going to drill a well, try to place it so you can build the cabin over it. Then you can install a hand pump inside the cabin and have water available without carrying it. This is especially agreeable during the winter.

Also, a completely automatic running water system can be built beyond electricity by using LP gas or a gasoline water pump equipped with a battery operated automatic starter.

Storage batteries to power many appliances, radios and television can be kept charged with wind chargers, gasoline engine driven generators or with solar cells. Solar cells are available from camper supply outlets that will keep a series of batteries charged. Provided, of course, that the sun shines for a reasonable amount of time on the area where you live.

You will probably have to use an outdoor toilet, but also can be kept heated, or at least be built so they offer good shelter.

With the present state of energy saving technology, there has never been a better time to take to the woods and take most of the comforts of civilization with you.

Figure 27.   Finished log cabin. Ready to move into.

Material List for Log Cabin

1.   Twenty-eight 12″ x 25′ logs for sidewall, or enough logs to build the walls 6 feet high. Extra logs are included to compensate for mistakes or ill fitting logs.

2.   Eleven 4″ x 23′ logs for floor joists. Substitute 2 x 10 planks if desired.

3.   Six 6″ x 24′ logs for pulins.

4.   Twenty-six 4″ x 12′ logs for rafters.

5.   Eight 12″ x 6′ logs for footing or calculate log lengths by depth of footings.

6.   400 square feet of flooring material.

7.   600 square feet of roof sheathing and roofing.

8.   Three windows and one door. Window size approximately 30″ x 38″. Door approximately 32 x 80.

9.   Five 12 foot 2 x 10's for window and door frames.

Chapter 6.

Erecting A Prefabricated Wilderness Cabin

Most people think of a log cabin when they think of a back-country dwelling, and rightly so, since it is picturesque and can be built from the materials at hand. However, when it comes to reality, the cabineer finds that it requires hard work, manual skill and plenty of building time. Further, in some areas where it would be desirable to live, few logs are available.

All of the fore-mentioned problems can be overcome, of course, but we have designed a cabin that can be cut out by the backyard builder while he is still in civilization. It can be trucked to the site with a pickup truck, ATV, snowmobile, canoes or boats or even horse and wagon. A helicopter pilot assures me he could fly the materials into a site with his "bird" also. It can be set and made ready to move into by two men in three to six days. It will pass the regulation for proving up a claim according to the Alaskan homestead laws, and perhaps most importantly, it will keep the occupate snug and warm during any winter found on the globe.

All the tools require to set it up are already owned by most, since about all that is needed is a handsaw, hammer and level. All intricate and laborious sawing is done in civilization where power equipment is available.

The first step in building even a pre-cut cabin is to carefully select the site. Spend plenty of time, preferably with your spouse or a companion, viewing the site from all angles. Be sure that the location you picked out won't be dangerous because large trees can fall on it, or be flooded if a nearby creek or lake raises it level. Make certain the site is well drained so puddles won't stand in your yard whenever it rains. Also, the availability of drinking water and sanitary facilities should be considered. In some places outdoor privies are illegal unless built according to a certain code. You also don't want to haul water too far if you are going to live full-time in the cabin.

Once the site is selected, stake out the corners and tie a string around the stakes to actually lay out the proposed walls. This often points out some overlooked faults, such as the poor view from the windows or uneven contour of the ground, that you can correct by moving the location a few feet.

The cabin can be supported on a footing foundation made by digging holes in the ground and setting wooden posts, concrete poured in a form or concrete blocks in the hole. In the latter case, the block cores are filled with wet concrete to create solid concrete footings.

The first step is to lay out the location for the holes. Since most buildings are aligned with the four directions, you can use a magnetic compass to lay out the first line of footings. This can be the north wall. A footing is set every 4 feet. First, drive the stake that will represent the northeast corner of the building. Tie a string to this stake and walk directly north for 20 feet and drive another stake. Tie a tight string between those stakes and you have a straight line for laying out the remaining four footings on the north wall.

Once the north wall stakes are set, the corners for the east and west must be set square with this line. An expedient way to do this is with the 6-8-10 method. Tie a string to a stake at the east end of the line of stakes just set. Use a carpenter's square to pull it at a 90 degree angle to the north wall. This will represent the east wall. Drive a stake 12 foot from the north wall stake and tie the string to it. Now measure 8 feet along the north wall and 6 feet along the east wall and mark the string for each measurement. The distance diagonally between the marks should be 10 feet. If it is not, adjust the east wall string until it is the correct distance. It will only require one stake for the east wall, and this will be in the center or at the 6 foot mark.

Use the same method for finding and squaring the south and west walls. A line of stakes also is placed down the center of the two outer walls for the intermediate footings. Now you can dig the holes and put the pillars in place. The footing excavations should be about 4 feet deep or down to firm soil. In some locations the entire cabin can be set on a rock shelf and only above ground supports are used.

Material List For Cabin Footings

Sixty 8 x 16 concrete blocks, or enough to extend from the depths of the footing excavation to 16″ above ground.

Six bags of Portland cement

½ yard of sand

½ yard of coarse aggregate

Twelve 8 foot reinforcing rod. Reinforcing rod is placed in the block cores.

Twelve ⅝ x 16 inch anchor bolts, or use ready bolts

Three 8 foot treated wooden posts for center supports, or Twelve 5 foot 4 inch 12 inch diameter treated wooden posts for perimeter footings.

Four 5 foot 4 inch 8 inch diameter treated wooden posts for center footings.

Poured concrete footings also can be used. Concrete forms must be used above ground. They can be built from scrap lumber for little cost. A poured concrete foundation will be more economical than using concrete blocks, but will require more labor.

After the holes are dug, set the concrete blocks in place. A single row of blocks are used. The cores are filled with wet

LAYOUT FOR FOOTINGS WITH SILLS IN PLACE

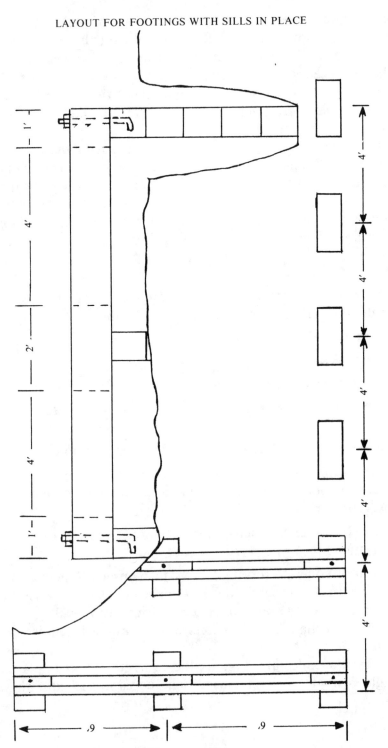

Figure 28.

concrete and a reinforcing rod is placed in each block core when the concrete is wet. An anchor bolt is also set in each footing on the perimeter. The anchor bolt is placed in the outside core of each footing.

Wooden supports can be made from replaced utility poles cut into the proper size. Many lumber yards or post yards will make them for you. Use pressure treated wood, if possible. They also can be made up from trees available on the site. In that case, brush on a good grade of commercial preservative or creosote. Use at least three coats after each has sunk in. Also use long lived wood such as white spruce or cedar if available. Adjust the top surface of each support so it is level with all the others. A line level and string is an expedient instrument for this task.

Cement footing should set at least a week before they are built on. Wooden supports can be used immediately. The next step is to put the sills in place. The sills are heavy wooden members that will support the floor joist. They are made from double lengths of 2 x 10 lumber spliced by sections of 2 x 10 blocking.

Material List For Sills

Twelve 6 foot 2 x 10's

Twelve 8 foot 2 x 10's

Obviously the 6 foot lengths can be made from three 12 foot board, but the 8 foot lengths are cut to produce twelve 6 foot board and six 2 foot boards and six 1 foot boards.

These can be cut out before hand or on the site. Each sill will be spliced with a 2 foot blocking piece in the center and a 1 foot blocking piece at each end.

The sills are laid across the footings and bolted to them with the anchor bolt. A ¾ inch diameter hole is drilled through the end blocking piece for the anchor bolt. When the sill is in place, a washer and nut is threaded on the anchor bolt and tightened. When wooden supports are used, the sills are spiked to the footing.

The next step is to put the floor joists in place. They are placed on 16 inch centers, a term that means they are 16 inches apart at the centerline. The floor joists are the members that the flooring is nailed on. They are placed at right angles to the sills.

Material List For Floor Joists

Twenty-three 8 foot 2 x 6's

Ten 4 foot 2 x 6's

These can be transported as 8 foot 2 x 6's and cut on the site if desired.

The joists are nailed to the sills using two 10d nails on each side of the joist at each sill. That will require about 320 nails or 5 pounds.

Be sure to stagger the joists so the 4 foot sections are not located at the same sill across the width of the floor. A row of blocking is placed at each end of the joists to close in the assembly. These are called the header joists.

After the floor joists are in place, the first layer of flooring can be put down. This subfloor is ½ inch CDX exterior grade plywood. This type of material is used when a second layer of plywood is placed over the top of the first layer. The second layer is also ½ inch plywood but it can be interior grade with one smooth sanded surface which is placed up towards the living space. The second layer of plywood called the underlayment, is not put down until the rest of the building is done.

FLOOR JOIST AND FLOORING LAYOUT
WITH JOISTS SPACED 16″ APART AND
4 x 8 PLYWOOD PANELING USED FOR
FLOORING

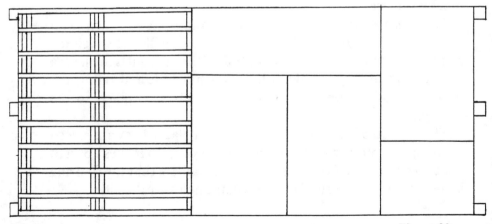

Figure 29.

Material List For The Underlayment

Eight sheets CDX ½″ x 4′ x 8′

The first layer is called the subfloor.

Eight sheets interior grade, one side sanded ½″ x 4′ x 8′ plywood

This second layer is called the underlayment.

16 pounds of 8d common nails

Lay the plywood so the joists are staggered. Nail it down by placing an 8d nail every 6 inches on the outside edges and every 10 inches on the intermediate joists.

The floor must be insulated with the insulation placed under the subfloor. The ideal insulation to use for this application is styrofoam plastic. Styrofoam comes in various thickness. Two inches of styrofoam plastic has a R value of 10, which should be adequate as long as the crawl space is enclosed.

This type of insulation can be ordered in 14½″ x 8′ sheets. Washer nails or roofing nails are used to nail it to the subfloor.

Material List For Floor Insulation

Twenty-three 14½ inch x 8 foot panels of styrofoam insulation

Two hundred 2½ inch roofing or washer nails

Take extra nails

The foam panels are placed between the floor joists and nailed in place. Place a nail every 12 inches, 2 inches from the outside boarder.

When the subfloor is laid, the wall construction can commence. The ceiling will be 7½ foot high. This is lower then the conventional ceiling for more efficient heating. The structure will have three windows in the south wall, one in the west wall. No windows are planned for the north or east wall. This is primarily for saving energy. If desired, windows can be put in the walls where they are lacking, simply by using the wall plan for installing the windows already shown.

The single door is located on the east end. It opens inward as do most exterior doors. An insulated steel door is used because it will provide maximum protection against bears in remote territories, and in not so remote country, it will withstand some forced entry attempts by human marauders. The windows should be fixed with 2 inch lumber shutters that fit tightly into the spaces provided on the windows for this. They are held in place with screws.

Material List For Walls

Full length studs. All full length studs are cut to 86 inches.

North wall

Twenty studs - includes both corners

West wall

Eleven studs - one window rough opening of 31-5/16 x 30 inches is provided in the west wall. *This rough opening can be provided between conventional 16 inch stud spacing. The studs on each side of the window opening are doubled. A double header is provided for the rough opening. This is fastened to the studding with framing anchors.*

Cripple studs are used over and under the rough opening. *Lower cripple studs are approximately 36 inches long and upper cripple studs are 12 inches long.*

Material List For South Wall

Seventeen studs

Three window rough openings are provided. *They are identical to the west wall window rough opening. The same size cripple studs are also used.*

Material List For East Wall

Eight full length studs - 83 x 37-½ inches long

A door rough opening needs two 83" trimmer studs, two 37-½ header pieces and two 3.5" cripple studs.

Cripple studs should be cut at the site since they might vary from the drawing because of construction errors.

Bottom plates, six 8 foot 2 x 4 - four 4 foot 2 x 4 includes all four walls.

Top plate, twelve 8 foot 2 x 4 - eight 4 foot 2 x 4 inlcudes all four walls.

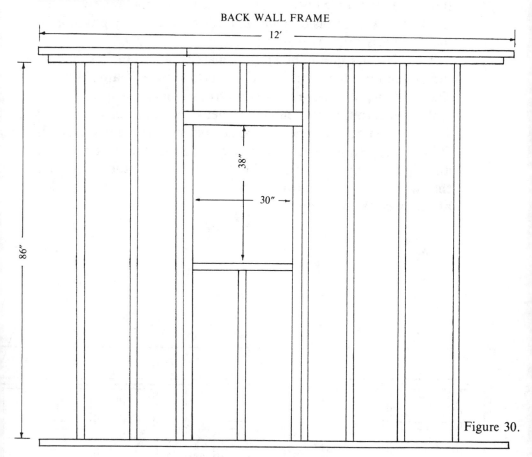

BACK WALL FRAME

Figure 30.

All saw cuts should be made very carefully to avoid poor fitting when the unit is assembled. Pile each group of cuts together and label them so they can be identified when you start to build.

The rough openings for the windows must be built into the wall when it is under construction. It can't be done before. Use double hung windows with insulated glass, if available. It is expected that storms and screens will be also obtained, and in many cases they come with the window accessories.

To form the south wall, all studs and cut to length and six 8 foot 2 x 4's are taken along to build the rough openings for the windows. The correct way to build a window rough opening is as shown on the drawing. First, the rough opening size must be figured. For double hung windows the rough opening size is the total glass width plus 6 inches and the total glass height plus 10 inches unless otherwise specified.

The windows should be approximately 34 x 28 inches, but the builder can use the nearest size that is available locally. For this size window, 38 x 30 inches is the rough opening size.

A 30 inch rough opening will fit between studs that are spaced 16 inches on center, since the space between these two studs is 30½ inches. Some space must be allowed to shim the window and square it up. It also should not bind on the studdings since that will cause the window to stick. The stud should be doubled at the window opening.

L. H. AND R. H. SIDEWALL FRAME   CORNER STUDS

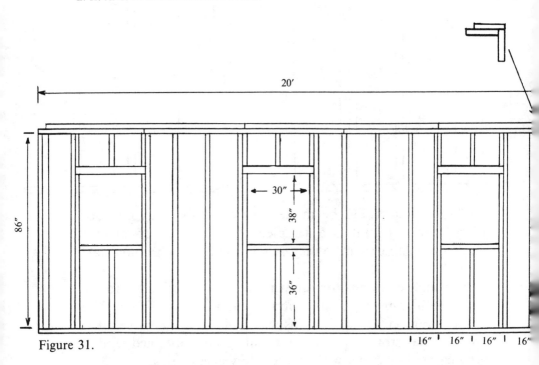

Figure 31.

Window rough openings are framed with a horizontal double 2 x 4 placed on edge between the two studs and a horizontal sill at the bottom. Cripple studs are used at the top and bottom of the windows.

The door will be a prehung metal door, measuring 32 x 80 inches. The rough opening size equals the width of the door plus 2½ inches, and the highest of the door plus 3 inches, so the rough opening must be 34½ inches wide. The height must be the door height plus 3 inches or 83 inches in this case.

However, the distance between the full length studs in the door rough opening is 37½ inches. This makes room for the side jambs, wedges and trimmer studs. It is well to cut the cripple and trimmer studs after the wall is in place.

FRONT WALL

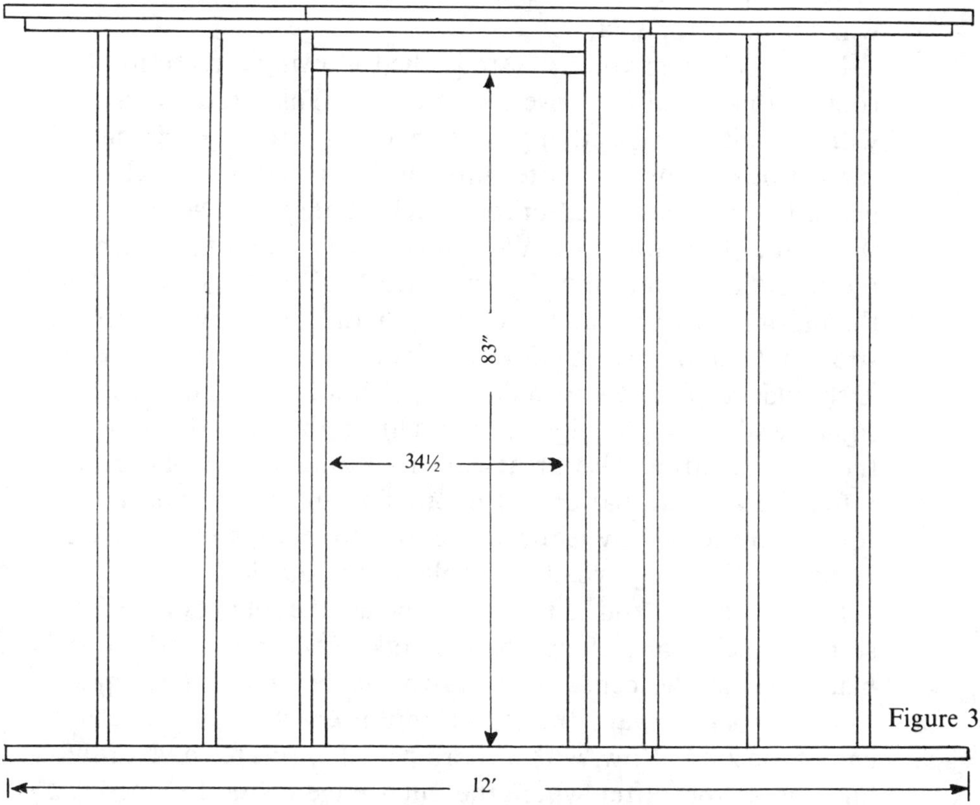

Figure 32.

A typical opening for use with a prehung door will have two trimmer studs, two head pieces and two cripple studs. The exact spacing will be determined by the dimensions given on the package or by the formula all ready mentioned. The distance inside the trimmer studs will be 34 inches. This allows ½ inch for the door frame to be wedged so the door will hang straight. The trimmer studs will be 83 inches long, the headers will be 37½ inches. Notice that the headers are supported by the trimmer studs. The cripple studs are 3.5 inches long.

After the sole plates, top plates, window frames and door frames and regular studding is in place, it is time to consider the ceiling and roof.

The rafters should be cut before hand. 2 x 6 inch stock is used for the rafters since they are spaced on 24 inch centers. It will require twenty-two 8 foot 2 x 6's to make the rafters. Cutting the rafters can be done by the home workman, or most lumber yards will cut them for you.

If you cut them yourself, study the following directions. The roof will have a 3 foot rise in the center. This produces a roof with a ¼ pitch. A ¼ pitch gives 6 inches of rise for each inch of span. Looking on the rafter table we find that a ¼ pitch roof needs 13.42 inches of rafter for each foot of span. The span is ½ the width of the building. We can find the rafter length without the overhang by multiplying 6 x 13.42 + 80.52 or 80½ inches. Cut the master rafter to the correct length and shape by selecting a straight 2 x 6 to use as a pattern. If it doesn't have a straight edge it should be planed or sanded to get it straight. Then use the square and a straight edge to draw a line right down the center of the pattern rafter. Use great care in all measurements on this rafter. Now lay the pattern rafter on a flat surface and take up the square so the narrow shorter section (tongue) is in your right hand and the long broad part (blade) in your left.

Start at the left end of the rafter and lay the square on the 2 x 6 so the 6 inch mark of the tongue and the 12 inch mark on the blade lay on the center line drawn on the rafter. The square should be slid toward the center until no part extends over the end of the 2 x 6. Now, with a sharp pencil or scratch awl, draw a line across the rafter where the outer edge of the tongue lays. This will mark the cut for the ridge board. Now, at the exact point where the pencil line intersects, the rafter center line, make a mark. Then measure from this mark along the centerline for 80.5 inches and make another mark. Then apply the square so the 12 inch mark on the blade intersects the center line at this point. Be sure the square is still held with the tongue in your right hand and the blade in your left. Now carefully mark the rafter along the blade. This will mark the cut for the top plate of the wall. Note that all the material above the centerline from the plate cut is left on the rafter for the overhang. This material is called the heel of the rafter. It is more expedient to nail them in place as they are and cut the ends of the heels off after the rafters are nailed in place and the roof sheathing applied.

Now make the saw cuts to form the rafter from the 2 x 6 board. Use great care in making this rafter since it is the pattern and all the rest are made from it. Saw the rafter at the lower end along the centerline to the intersection with the plate mark. Then make the cut from the centerline to the lower edge of the rafter to form the seat for the plate. The upper end of the rafter is cut back ¾ inch from the ridge board cut because of the thickness of the ridge board. This forms the pattern rafter, and it is used for a direct patter for making the other twenty-one rafters. To use the pattern rafter for marking the rest, just lay the pattern right on the 2 x 6 and use a scratch awl to mark the ridge board cut, the plate cut and rafter tail.

RAFTER AND GABLE STUD LAYOUT

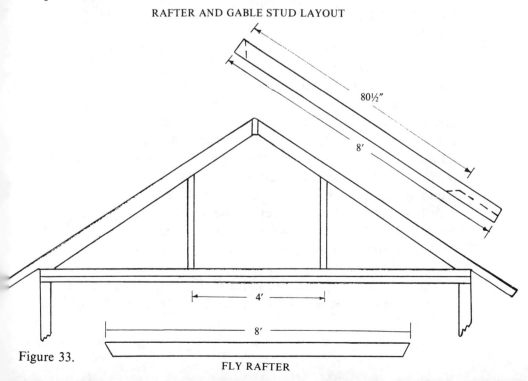

80½"

8'

4'

8'

Figure 33.

FLY RAFTER

After the rafters are cut, they should be tied into bundles with five in a bundle. This will leave one bundle with only two rafters in it. Put the ridge boards in this bundle. This will require three 8 foot 2 x 6's. The surplus 2 feet of ridge board is used for the scab splices where the ends of the ridge board meet.

The roof sheathing material can be ½ inch exterior grade plywood or the equivalent. It will require ten 4 x 8 sheets of ½ inch plywood for the sheathing. Depending upon the mode of transportation, the physical size of 4 x 8 sheets might be a problem. It is expected that they will be cut into 2 x 8 sheets if needed. Do not cut them into 4 x 4 sheets as problems will be encountered when laying the sheets since they won't reach between the rafters in some instances. The roof sheath should all be put in one pile with the rafters.

The rafters are nailed to the ridge board with two 10d nails on each side of the rafter. Using the formula, twelve pounds of nails per 1,000 board feet of lumber, it will require approximately 2½ pounds of 10d nails for the rafters. The roof sheathing will require approximately four pounds of 8d nails. A nail is placed every 6 inches on the edges and every foot on the rafters where the edge of the sheathing does not meet. Be sure to stagger the ends of the plywood so all the seams are not located on one rafter.

Thirty pound felt underlayment and ninety pound roll mineral surface roofing will be used for sealing the roof. It will require four rolls of each when the roofing is purchased in 100 square feet rolls. It is expected that the roofing will be overlaid or lapped 3 inches, as is standard. It will require four pounds of 1 inch galvanized roofing nails to nail down each layer. All roofing materials should be put in one area for counting as they are purchased. It will require four items to make the roof. The rafter, wooden roof sheathing, roll roofing and nails.

When the building is erected, the walls will be put up and braced, then the work on the roof will commence. The sooner the roof is on the less damage from rain that will occur. Install the ceiling joists at this time.

The next item to consider is the wall siding. This building is built to take advantage of the structural strength that will be

PRE-FAB CABIN UNDER CONSTRUCTION

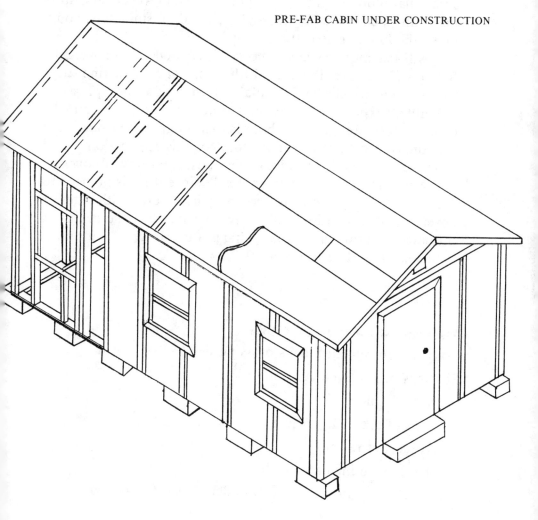

Figure 34.

realized with ½ inch, 4 x 8 plywood panels. Nail vertical 1 x 2 furring strips on 24 inch centers to the siding to create a board and batten effect.

If the builder wants to substitute 4 x 8 sheets of commercial siding, it will work fine. The minus factors are, more cost and somewhat more weight to transport. Don't, however, substitute insulating board and horizontal strip siding since this would make the building structurally weakened.

It will also require sixteen sheets of plywood and forty-eight 8 foot 1 x 2's to cover the walls. Either 1 x 2 or 1 x 3 furring strips can be used, whichever is available locally at a good price.

Paint all exposed wood as soon as possible after setting up the cabin. Most composition boards, although somewhat more economical, will not be satisfactory for this application.

The gable ends will require gable studs, exterior wall covering and vents. They are made from 2 x 4's since there is no need to use 2 x 6's. The gable ends need only be covered with exterior covering, no insulation will be needed inside if the ceiling is insulated. If a cathedral type ceiling is used, the gable ends must be insulated and be finished off.

Material list for Pre-Fab Cabin

Sixty 8 x 16 cement blocks or as needed

Six bags of Portland cement

½ yard of sand

½ yards of coarse aggregate

Twelve 8 foot re rods

Twelve ⅝ x 16 inch anchor bolts

Three 10 x 8 inch treated wooden posts for center footings

or

Twelve 12″ x 5′4″ treated posts for perimeter footings.

Four 8″ x 5′4″ treated wooden posts.

Floor Sills

twelve 6 foot 2 x 10's

twelve 8 foot 2 x 10's

Floor Joists

Twenty-nine 8 foot 2 x 6's

Five pounds 10d nails

Flooring

Eight sheets ½ x 4' x 8' CDX plywood for subfloor

Eight sheets ½ x 4' x 8' interior grade (sanded one side) for underlayment.

Sixteen pounds 8d common nails

Floor Insulation

Twenty-three 2" x 14½" x 8' styrofoam panels

Five pounds 2¼" roofing nails or washer nails.

Wall Frames

Fifty-six 8 foot 2 x 4's cut to 86 inches.

Window Frames

Twelve 8 foot 2 x 4's to be cut to size after windows are purchased.

Door Frame

Two 8 foot 2 x 4's cut to 83 inches

One 37½ inch 2 x 4

Rafters

Twenty-two 8 foot 2 x 6's

Two 12 foot 2 x 6's for ridgeboard

Ceiling Joists

Eleven 12 foot 2 x 6's

Roof Sheathing

Ten sheets ½ x 4' x 8' CDX plywood or the equivelant

Roofing

Four rolls 30# felt underlayment

Four rolls 90# mineral surface roofing

Eight pounds 1 inch galvanized roofing nails

Siding

Sixteen sheets ½ x 4 x 8' CDX plywood panels for siding.

Twenty pounds 16d galvanized siding nails.

Gables

Two 8 foot 2 x 4's cut to length on the site

Five sheets ½ x 4' x 8' CDX plywood for siding

Vents

Screened vents should be used when a ceiling is built into the structure.

Sixteen sheets 1" x 4" x 8' styrofoam insulation paneling.

This is placed under the siding on the outside walls.

240 square feet of 6 inch thick fiberglass insulation for the roof.

Ceiling covering and interior paneling is to be selected by the builder. If a flat ceiling is desired, it will require about 240 square feet of ceiling material. The insulation should be placed over the ceiling. In this case a layer 12 inches thick can be used.

Chapter 7.

Getting Fresh Meat

Settle in almost any backcountry area in the states covered in this book and you should be able to get most of your fresh meat by cropping the surplus game animals and birds, within a short distance of your cabin. A big game rifle, a .22 rifle and a shotgun will provide all the guns needed for hunting. Some people prefer to trap rabbits and other small game, and at least two live traps, well set, will keep the family in rabbit and squirrel meat.

The whitetail deer has kept many a backwoods family in delicious meat, and will continue to do so. The cabineer should thoroughly acquaint himself with the habits of the whitetail, and just as importantly he should develop an intimate knowledge of the terrain surrounding his cabin, because he will likely be hunting for a special strain of deer that I call the north woods deer. They are much more wary and harder to bag than farmland deer.

North woods deer populations are as low as five to the square mile, and it is necessary to understand some of their habits to

Figure 35.   An elk can furnish meat for the winter.

consistently bag your meat. Often backcountry populations consist of three to five year old doe who is the mother and natural leader, her pair of fawns from this season and a spike buck and yearling doe who are her progency from the previous season. Usually there is also a mature buck or two, but they keep to themselves except in rutting season.

The deer stay within unmarked boundaries of a section of terrain that they think of as home territory. This section has to include a variety of prime feeding locations, such as cutover areas, backwoods clearings, alder swamps and young aspen. Somewhat surprisingly, the deer follow about the same paths when they travel from one feeding area to another.

These paths might not be the distinct deer trails that are found in the southern counties where deer might number 25 to 36 animals to the square mile. Instead they are faint marks which usually follow contours or lines of dense vegetation.

Backwoods deer trails can often be found in a pass through a line of ridges, a wooden point extending into an open marsh, natural river or creek fords or a line of short thick conifirs through a stand of large hardwoods. Locate these trails and you can return to them year after year as long as the forest cover remains. They are excellent places for permanent or temporary ground or tree blinds.

If you can find oak tree stands in your territory, be sure to hunt them because when the acorns mature and start falling to the ground, the does and small bucks will nearly abandon all other food stuff and gorge themselves with this nutritious mast. This creates a layer of fat to fortify the animal against the winter, and it also creates delicious tasting venison.

Most of the acorns fall in late September and early October, but this depends on the weather. However, this feast only lasts about two weeks in most northern areas because stands of oaks are scarce and the acorns quickly eaten.

The best way to hunt this food source is to select a stand on the route the deer are using to approach the oak stand. They seldom bed under the oaks, favoring instead a nearby conifir stand or alder choked lowland for a bedding ground. Often they follow about the same route from bed to board each afternoon. For the

Figure 36.   Bowhunting can keep the cabineer in meat. The author is shown
with a whitetail buck.

duration of the feast of the acorns, the north woods hunter has about the best chance of the year for bagging a deer.

However, the larger bucks don't seem to trouble themselves to leave their customary haunts just for acorns. Instead they become most vulnerable when the rut starts and they start making scrapes.

A buck scrape is a triangular shaped depression in the ground where all the vegetation is scraped away down to bare found. It is made as a sign that he is ready to breed. Bucks make this scrape with their forefeet, they also plant one hoof print in the middle of the scrape. They further scent the scrape by urinating over their hocks so the urine runs over the hock gland and carries scent into the scrape. Often the scrape is located on an overhanging branch that the buck chews and rubs with the glands located under his eyes.

The deer hunter might suppose that he could watch a buck scrape and sooner or later the deer would come to it. However, this can be unproductive for several reasons. First, he makes more scrapes then he watches, therefore, he might never come back to the one you are watching. Even if he does come by, he might approach it from downwind and scent the hunter before he can get a shot. Consequently, it is better to set up an ambush along the route the buck uses to patrol his scrape. Usually the male deer will patrol his route by staying in the thickest cover available.

Sometimes it is possible to find his faint trail through these areas, and there are always natural obstructions such as ridges and clearings which will guide him into a possible ambush. Ambush sites are based on natural obstructions are often useful year after year because succeeding generations of bucks use about the same scrape routes when rutting in the same place.

Where legal, tree stands are far and away the most productive for this type of hunting since they allow the hunter to see the animal coming better, and the extra height disperses the scent to a greater extent then if then the hunter was on the ground. Don't depend on a rutting buck doing something foolish, even though stories of foolish rutting bucks abound. They don't make many mistakes.

Although some of the deer scents in use today may have some value, the very best way to counteract the deer's nose is to keep yourself as scent free as possible. Leave your hunting clothes outside or if you bring them inside, put them in a bag with some cedar boughs, sweet fern or other strong smelling natural product that will permeate the cloth with a natural odor. If possible, bathe just before you go hunting. Use baking soda or plain water instead of scented soap and skip the shave. Don't eat onions, peanut butter or carry highly scented foods with you. Don't use deodorants, don't smoke or chew gum and try not to work up a sweat getting to your stand.

I have followed these practices and I find I can make myself scent free enough so a deer will approach within 25 yards before winding me. Even then they might go through an alarm ritual of throwing up their head and switching their tail before they flee. This usually gives the alert hunter enough time for a shot.

Even after you have found a good stand or trail to watch, there is a possibility the deer will temporarily abandon the "highway" for several reasons. If it is the buck he might find an receptive doe and follow her wherever she goes until she is bred. If deer are using the trail to find a food source, they might change menus and a period of unusually wet or dry weather might influence their movements. When the ground is carpeted with a thick coating of leaves, it is extremely hard to see tracks, and so the hunter might watch an unused trail for several fruitless days.

Keep this from happening by scraping the leaves away in a large enough area so any deer walking by will make tracks in the bare soil. By doing this everyday, an amazing amount of information can be gathered. You tell about how many deer are in the area, what direction they usually come from when they approach the area. The approximate size and sex, because a large lone deer in the fall is often a buck. Nearly every doe has a fawn by her side.

After you have proved your stand is a good one, and the area is being used by deer, it is time to call on the quality that is almost indispensable to the food gathering big woods deer hunter . . . the willingness to stay quietly on your stand through all sorts of weather and hours. Call it patience or call it confidence, the ability to stay quietly in one place will put more deer within your range then any other single factor, especially in the deep woods where a few other hunters are about to move the deer.

When you first take to the woods, you might be too "hyper" to be able to set in one place for a long time, but it is a skill that can be learned. The best way to keep yourself on your stand is to have unflagging confidence in your location. Then when you are hunting, think deer. Listen and watch very closely, and you will probably be surprised how many animals and birds are nearby. This will help take the edge off the boredom of long waits.

Most of the Lower 48 states have an archery season that lasts much longer then the gun season, and offers hunting that is neither crowded or hurried, and therefore provides an excellent

Figure 37.   The author with a whitetail buck bagged in northern Wisconsin.

chance for the cabin dweller to get his winter's meat. Also, many people believe deer meat is better tasting if taken early in the season before the rut starts.

In the western states, mule deer are the predominant deer, white tails existing only in a few areas. Therefore, mule deer offer in some cases the best source of wild meat to the cabin dweller.

Mule deer hunting for big bucks has changed somewhat in the last 20 years. These days the bucks have been hunted enough so they don't stand around on the hillsides looking at the hunter the way they use to. Now it is necessary to look for them in the draws and pockets where they bed down in heavily wooded territory. Maybe the best way to get a mule deer buck is to get up on the side of the ridges before daylight in the morning and watch for one to move from his feeding grounds to his bedding location.

The use of a spotting scope or a pair of binoculars is almost mandatory, since deer are often spotted a mile away or more. Once the buck is spotted, watch him until you see him lay down and then stalk him. Stay downwind during the stalk, stay below the skyline of ridges if possible, and be prepared to take a long shot.

When hunting alone during the midday, when deer are likely to be bedded down for the day, many hunters walk the tops of ridges and roll rocks down into the ravines between the ridges. This commotion will often get a deer to its feet.

Don't ignore the weather when mule deer hunting either. They like to stay comfortable, and on a cold day but clear day, they will often be on the sunny or south side of the mountain in the mornings. In the evenings after they have soaked up their quota of sunshine, and the weather may be too warm for them, they will often move to the shady or north side of the mountain. When a cold front moves in, the deer will go to the top of the mountain, but if there is high wind with the cold front, they will be on the protected side of the mountain, out of the wind.

After the moutain is covered with snow, mule deer will tend to concentrate about ½ way up the slope on the sunny side. On dark and cloudy days they tend to stay near the bottom of brushy protected ravines close to a source of water. If snow is falling at dawn, spend the morning stalking low saddles along the easiest routes between two ridges. From noon until dark, move to the northside of the mountain.

However, probably more mule deer are killed by hunters that get out before dawn and watch trails and feeding areas then any other way. Just before dark is also a major time to see mule deer. To get the best ducks, get as far off the road as you can.

Black bear are found in both the east, midwest and west, as well as in the far north, and chances are good if you settle in the deep woods there will be black bear nearby. They are excellent eating if taken when fat in the fall, or just as they emerge from their dens in the early spring.

It comes as a surprise that bears are still fat when they come out of their winter sleep in the spring, and don't become thin until they start moving around, providing they were fat when they went into hibernation. The first thing a bear does when it emerges in the spring is to start drinking water. All the water is can hold. This seems to start the digestive organs working, which have shrunk greatly during their months of disuse.

Then bears start looking for food. If available, they will feed heavily on carrion. This seems to be an instinctive need to replenish their protein supplies. When they can't get carrion, they substitute on grass, catkins of plants and in particular, aspen leaves when they are small. Where I hunt, patch of white clover are heavily browsed by black bear.

Where spring hunting seasons are open, a good way to get a bear is to watch mountain meadows or emerging patches of green grass or stands of aspen. Usually bear defecate quite heavily when eating grass, and if they have been feeding steadily in one place, their sign will be easy to find.

Black bear also frequent streams where they can catch spawning suckers, salmon or other fish in the spring. The headwaters, in particular of such streams, are good places to watch for bear since the water is usually shallow and the fish are easier for the bear to catch.

Where baiting is legal, as it is most states and provinces, black bear can be baited with large meat objects, such as beaver carcasses left over from the winter trapping season. Most baiters place about 5 to 10 pounds of meat in a bag and hang it in a tree

Figure 38.   A black bear can furnish many pounds of good meat. This
hunter is named Ray Bray, and the bear is the biggest black
ever killed in Michigan.

someplace near water and heavy cover where bears are sure to frequent. After he has hit the same bait twice, a larger bait is usually established nearby.

A good bear bait is a 50 gallon steel drum filled with beaver meat. A hole is cut in the top about 1 foot in diameter. This barrel is wired to a tree to keep the bear from tipping it over. The bear then reaches into the hole to get the bait out with his paw. This keeps him from eating it all at once. A bait like this will keep a bear or two coming back for a month or more in the spring. The hunter usually sets in a nearby blind waiting for the bear. They often come in the evening.

Another bait that bears find attractive is whole corn, wheat or oats with restaurant deep fat grease poured over it. Restaurants have to change this oil every so often and usually will give it away. Grain also is effective if coated with sugar water that has some anise flavoring added to it. Baiting is effective in the fall as well as in the spring.

Where bear baiting is not legal, most hunters watch areas where bear come into stands of cherry trees, apple trees, acorn bearing oak trees or other high energy food. Bears feed heavily all summer and early fall, building up a layer of fat that is often 5 inches thick or more.

Cabineers who settle in the western states or provinces will have access to elk hunting. The elk is a challenging beast to hunt, and its antlers make the most impressive wall hanging of any animal. The skin also is very useful after being tanned. Moreover, elk meat is considered by many to be the finest meat of all game animals.

Elk spend the summer high in the mountains, where the weather is cool and the flies aren't so troublesome. As deep snow falls they work down the mountains, and in many cases spend the winters in huge elk yards.

In the early fall when elk season first opens, they are still high, and the hunter must go after them. They might be miles from the nearest road, and most of the going more of less up the mountain. If available, horses are far and away the best way to travel in the mountains. A mounted rider can cover much more territory

Figure 39.   A bull elk coming to a call.

in a day than a man on foot, especially if you have considerable gear.

However, unless you live in elk country and have a saddle horse, getting the horse to the territory where you want to start hunting, as well as caring for him afterward, is also a hassle. Therefore, many very good hunters hunt elk on foot and manage to get elk nearly every year. These hunters are in good shape, they are knowledgeable hunters, and most camp out right in the hunting territory that they are going to hunt. After they bag an elk, they either carry it out on their own or hire a packer to get it out for them.

Once in elk territory, you have a choice of methods to use, but bugling is one of the most dramatic and interesting ways to get close to them. In this method, the hunter gets out well before dawn and listens for a bull to start bugling. An elk bugling sounds a little like someone blowing on a flute, with a sound of a donkey braying at the end. This is usually followed by a few grunts. Once heard, it is never forgotten. It is fairly easy to learn to bugle an elk. I learned how to call them without ever hearing a live elk. Just by listening to tapes. I believe most anyone can.

Elk bugles are available commercially, or they can be homemade of plastic or steel tubing. Diaphram calls are starting to get popular. A large plastic tube about 4 feet long and 3 to 4 inches in diameter can be used to amplify the sound when you want it to carry a long ways.

Once you hear a bull elk, get as close to him as you can before you start bugling. After he answers, take a dead stick and thrash it around in the brush so it sounds like a bull elk fighting branches. Bull elk do this to get themselves worked up enough to fight. When another hears this sound he often gets enraged and will come running. Be sure you are well concealed so he doesn't see you and he will probably come in. Some come in fast, and some sneak around, coming in very quietly.

Stalking or still hunting is also very widely used by unmounted hunters. In this case the hunter walks slowly and carefully through areas where elk are likely to be bedded or up feeding. If there is snow on the ground, the hunter watches enough to get up on the herd before it sees or winds him.

Elk often bed down in thick stands of timber where fallen and criss-cross timber makes a quiet approach very difficult. However, with considerable practice and a little luck, bedded elk can be approached, especially if they aren't too spooky.

When following tracks in the snow, the elk hunter spends alot of time glassing the area ahead and on all sides so he sees the elk before they see him. Once the elk are spotted, a stalk is made that will keep the hunter downwind from the animals and out of sight as much as possible. In some areas, elk have trails as distinct as cow trails, and if you can find such a location, try hunting out of a tree stand or on a ridge overlooking the trail for best results.

Elk are certainly a huge animal, and when you down one you have a good supply of meat, maybe even enough to last all winter, but cabineers who live in the far north, and even in some of the Lower 48 states can hunt the mighty moose. One moose could furnish enough meat for a family.

Moose seasons open in August in some areas, and in September and October for most of them. Moose are hunted along waterways to a great extent, since that is where they spend most of their time. A favorite way to hunt moose in Ontario and in some other areas is, to canoe quietly along the shoreline of a lake or river and watch closely for a sight of their large dark body feeding in the shallows. Sometimes moose are feeding on aquatic plants in water 10 feet deep or more, and they dive to the bottom, seize a mouthful of food and bob back up again to eat it. They usually feed in water less then 6 feet deep though, but even then the only visible portion of their body is a dark hump on the water. A sight easy to miss if the hunter is looking for the whole body of the moose.

However, in most cases the moose will quickly see the hunter and flee. Happens you do find a moose out in the lake feeding, hug the shoreline with your canoe and get as close as possible. Swimming moose shouldn't be shot, but when he sees you and takes off for the bush, he's legal game once he reaches dry land, and if you are ready you can get in at least one good shot. A method that is particularly successful for approaching a feeding moose is to move only when he has his head underwater.

Many moose are bagged from dry land also. If you can find a favorite feeding area for moose, watch in the evening for them to come out of the forest to feed, or for them to come out to the lake in the evening, or they can be spotted on mountain sides, or along the sideroads. Then stalk them.

When stalking moose, as with all game animals, stay downwind from them and stay very quiet. Move only when the animal isn't looking at you, and move slowly then.

After the snow falls, moose can be stalked with a little more success, since their tracks can be spotted and you know about where they are located. I like to follow a moose until it gets into a thick stand of balsam or into a thick alder swamp. Then I circle the swamp to see if the moose came out. If it didn't, I will carefully follow the tracks to see if I can get a shot when it jumps up.

Moose often circle and bed down so they are downwind from their trail. This so if a hunter comes into the thicket on his track, he will wind the hunter before the hunter can see him. Even so, if you follow quietly and watch closely, you might get a good shot when it jumps up. This will happen for several reasons. One that the breeze and air currents are fickle and even though you are directly upwind he might not wind you until you are very close.

Another that he might know you are coming but won't move because he hopes he is hidden and you will walk by.

If you can find a companion to hunt with you, this type of a setup is ideal for a drive. Find out where the moose is bedded and post one hunter at one end of the thicket and walk in the other, following its tracks. When it jumps out and runs it will probably run by the first hunter as he is posted on a likely trail or escape route. On snowy days, moose often move around right during the day also, and you might spot one, especially if you get on a moose trail.

During the rut many hunters can call the bull moose by making the sound of a love sick cow moose. This is an easily imitated sound that to my ear resemble the mooing of a domestic cow. Rutting bull moose also fight brush and trees at this time of the year, and trample down large areas, sometimes completely destroying the vegetation in a house sized area.

Combining canoe hunting along rivers or lakes with calling moose is a very intriguing way to hunt. First, find an area where a bull in rut is located. This can be done by listening for his call or by finding the wallows or rubs made on trees. Then paddle quietly into the area before dawn and when it gets daylight, start calling. Don't call too frequently, but call loudly three or four times and then wait about 15 to 20 minutes before calling again. Occassionally pour water into the lake to imitate the sound of a moose urinating in the water, or if on shore, break branches by picking up a dead stick and thrashing it about like a bull fighting trees.

If the bull answers, call in response to his calling, but again don't call so often he gets suspicious. Watch very closely for him to come in. Until you have seen it you can't believe how quietly a huge animal like a moose can move.

A .308, 3006, 7mm or heavier caliber rifle is a good choice for a moose. Tools needed for handling a downed bull include a sharp knife or two and a sharpening stone. A small axe and 50 feet of rope. A small hoist is also handy, if you have one. Experienced moose handlers can gut and quarter a large bull in an hour or so, providing they can get him laid on his back so the guts an be removed.

Caribou are another animal that can be depended upon to

furnish protein to the settler who makes his home where they live. Barren land caribou usually live in herds and migrate long distances between the winter and summer calving grounds. There are twelve large caribou herds in Alaska, and some cross the Alaskan Highway when migrating, which brings them into range of many bush dwellers. Caribou are not known as a wary animal, and the main problem in collecting them is to get where they are at the time you want one. Most of the time they are miles from the nearest road and are hard to approach, except by floatplane or boat.

While big game animals are the mainstay of bush dwellers everywhere, in some places considerable meat can be obtained by hunting small game and birds and waterfowl. In the far north, ptarmigan, spruce grouse, snowshoe hare and waterfowl help many a bushman with his winters meat.

In the Lower 48, even the northern states covered in this book, gray squirrels, cottontail rabbits, grouse and even pheasant abound in some areas and can be utilized to whatever extent the person wants.

Chapter 8
Fishing For Food

Probably most cabin dwellers will take care to locate their homestead close to a river, lake, pond or ocean. Indeed, it would be hard not to be close to a body of water in the states and provinces that are included in this book, since there are so many.

Most water has a fish population, but a few lakes don't, and some research will indicate whether the lake you are considering has a good and varied fish population before you build. Once you have settled in and are beginning to get your food from the land, fish can be an important part of your food supply.

Fish can be frozen, smoked, canned or dried to preserve them, and they also can be pickled for a taste treat. However, don't forget if you live on a good fishing lake you can get fish the year around. They bite in winter as well as in summer, and many times winter fishing is more productive than summer fishing.

In the Lower 48 states, and in some sections of Canada where warm water lakes are abundant, the bluegill is a good fish to consider for a reliable food source. It is impossible to fish them

out by hook and line fishing, and they will bite nearly everyday, the year around.

Bluegills usually live in schools, and they often stay in about the same places in a lake, creating what is sometimes called a bluegill bed. Once these beds are found, they can be fished summer and winter with good results. But in the spring, as soon as the water warms up, the bluegills move in from the depths to the shallows to spawn. Several days before they spawn they will be holding in the shallows. When they are at this stage they will bite as well as they do all year.

A productive way to catch them is with a light spin fishing rig, using angleworms for bait. Keep well back from the area that you want to fish to avoid spooking them. The bobber should be set about a foot from the hook so the bait dangles well off the bottom. Cast out into the middle of the fish. The splash of the bobber hitting the water usually attracts any nearby bluegills, and they often bite as fast as you throw the bait in the water. However, they can only see a short distance, so be sure to get the bait into the school.

Some cabineers lay in a years supply of fillets at this time. After the spawning season, bluegills will still take floating poppers and other flies every readily. Use a canoe or row boat to cruise near banks in the evening and cast to the shoreline.

On the days when they don't take a popper readily, try the dropper line set-up. A dropper line is created by tying a foot-long section of light line into the eye of the popper. A #10 hook is baited with fish worm is bent to the other end of the line so when the lure is cast into the water the popper floats on the surface, but allows the baited hook to dangle above the shallow weed beds where the bluegills are apt to be hiding. This is effective because it appeals to the bluegills visual instinct to watch the surface for movement, and to his sense of smell for bait. It is common when they are biting good to get a bluegill on the popper and one on the dropper line at the same time.

When the heat of the summer warms the upper surface of the water to over 75 degrees, the larger bluegills seek the depths where the suns rays aren't quite so bright on his sensitive eyes and the temperature is more to his liking. Often they congregate in huge schools in these sections of preferred habitat. They are hard to catch because they bite very delicately. They are often suspended 20 to 30 feet below the surface where few people even try for them. Many people think big bluegills don't even bite in midsummer.

However, this trick will take them. Put some light monofiliment line on your spinning reel. Use #3 pound test if available. Use #10 thin wire hook and two split shot. Go to a lake or pond where there is a known good population of bluegills. Bait the hook with a short piece of angleworm, wax worm, mousies or other small grub. It is important to keep the bait small. Use the depth finder or anchor to find a place at least 30 feet deep. Drop the line over the side until you are fishing just above the bottom. Attach a small bobber at this depth. The bobber should be very small so that you can detect the slightest bite. Watch the bobber closely, and if it moves even slightly, set the hook.

It might take sometime to find the fish, but when you do you can return time after time to the same place. Usually on cloudy days the bluegills will be somewhat shallower than on bright days.

In areas where the fishing laws will permit, bluegills can be seined very effectively, especially when they are in the shallows in the spring. With a sein you can usually catch several dozen at a time. Also, they can be caught in a large funnel trap made like a large minnow trap. The key is to use oderous bait. This funnel trap also works very well for catching bullheads and catfish, two other fish that can supply many pounds of fillets to the food fishermen.

As soon as the water warms up to about 60 degrees, the bullheads and catfish become actively feeding. In spring they are good eating. Not so later in the year when they often develop a muddy flavor. The main ingredients in catching either of these two fish is to have a good natural bait and fish in the evening or at night when they are the most active.

Almost any tackle will be effective for bullhead fishing, and millions have caught on a cane pole rigged with heavy cotton line and large hooks baited with angleworms or cheese baits.

Another prolific fish found in warm water lakes is the northern pike. The northern is found all over the U.S., Alaska and Canada, and he is usually hungry. Most people cast spoons or fish with minnows, but the most successful northern fisherman that I have ever known used bluegills for bait. He impaled the bluegill on a large treble hook with one hook paused under the dorsal fin of the bluegill. He also clipped off part of the dorsal fin of the bluegill. This seemed to make the bait fish more apt to draw a strike because it swam erratically. Predatory fish, like the northern, are more likely to hit a crippled fish because it looks like an easy meal. He slow trolled this bait by projecting his pole from the back of the boat and rowing around the lake, usually in the morning and evening hours. He used 100 pound test line and a bamboo pole. When he got hit from an extremely large northern, he threw the pole over the back of the boat into the water and then rowed around behind the fish as it towed the pole around until it tired itself out. When it looked like most of the fight was gone out of the northern, he picked up his pole and brought in the fish. He caught more large northerns than all the rest of the fishermen together in the village that he lived in.

Although large bait fish are good bait, sometimes the northerns will bite best on dare devil type spoons, and I imagine more are caught on large spinners than any other type of lure. But, after four decades, I have proved to myself at least, that fishing with minnows, frogs or other natural bait will catch more fish on a day in and day out basis than artificial lures.

In most places it is legal to fish with two or more lines at the same time, so put all the odds in your favor by fishing with artificial baits with one line and natural baits with the other. In this way you can find out what baits will produce best on a particular day.

Where legal, northerns can be speared quite successfully. Many spearmen walk the banks or paddle slowly around the lake looking down into the water until they spot a resting northern. The polaroid type of sun glasses help alot with this. A long handled spear is pushed very slowly down through the water until it is a few inches from the fish. Then a quick thrust impales the fish. Although spears are equipped with barbs, the

Figure 41.　A large northern pike will gladden the heart of any fisherman and supply considerable food for the table.

fish will often get away if the spearman can't hold the fish against the bottom. If you don't hold the fish against the bottom, drop the spear handle so the fish can take it with him during the few short frantic lunges it makes immediately after being speared. When spearing large fish, use a spear with a slip handle. With this set-up the spear head is fastened to a line and the fisherman plays the fish like a hook and line fisherman. He must be careful not to pull hard enough to jerk the spear out of the quarry.

Walleyes are also a favorite food fish, and in many areas like northern Minnesota, they are the most popular game fish. Walleyes are more of a bottom feeder than northern pike, so lead head jigs are probably most popular lure, either tipped with a minnow or a strip cut from the belly of a fish. Fishing for them is nearly the same as fishing for northerns except they tend to bit on smaller minnows, are more attracted to slower moving lures and they feed more at night.

The walleyes have large eyes that are coated with a covering that attracts light, and therefore they are adapt at seeing in very dim light. They spend the brightest part of the day in deep water or hiding under vegetation to avoid the light. But, just before sunset they often cruise into the shallows to catch and eat minnows that live along the shorelines.

For this reason (where legal) set lines (sometimes called trot lines) are very adaptable for catching these fish. A 75 foot set line, equipped with two dozen hooks set out from the shoreline will usually produce all the fish a family can eat. Use night crawlers, leeches and small minnows for bait. Of course, many cabineers would rather catch them one at a time on spinning tackle.

If you settle down on the shore of the Great Lakes, you will have access to water darkening millions of rough fish to harvest. Smelt come to the shorelines to spawn in early spring. They are harvested with dip nets and seines, and in most years every fishermen will get as many as he feels he can use. Smelt are very nutritious fish, and they can be frozen, canned, pickled and smoked to preserve them.

Red horse and suckers are another fish that make themselves very available to fishermen in early spring when they are spawning. They can be taken in large dip nets, speared, caught in fish traps and even caught by hand. In some places they are snagged by dragging a weighted snagging hook through the shallows where they congregate. Suckers have a good flavor even though they are bony. They make good pickled fish because the vinegar softens the bones. They also make good smoked fish or canned fish.

Many people will settle where they can subsist on white fish, trout and salmon. Both fish are excellent eating. They also are very widely distributed and become available in the shallows only during certain seasons. In many places they can be dip netted, especially during the fall spawning season when they come to the surface. Fishermen paddle around the lake shining a flashlight in the water until they spot one. Then they approach very slowly and dip them out with a dip net.

In early winter, as soon as the lake freezes, but before the snow falls, whitefish can sometimes be seen cruising along underneath ice at night. The spearman operate in pairs. After the direction of the fish is ascertained, one spearman goes ahead and chops a hole in the ice. The other then pounds on the ice and tries to herd the fish towards the hole. The whitefish is speared when he comes to the hole in the ice. I have participated in this activity, and it is a thrill a minute. Made more thrilling by the possibility that you will fall through the thin ice any minute.

Probably the all time best method of catching trout and whitefish was passed on to me by an elderly Norwegian fisherman who lives on the shores of Lake Superior in Michigan's Upper Peninsula. If you have a good fish population in your lake and you can get the bait, no problem will be found in catching your years supply during the spring and early summer using this buoy and bait method.

First, find a fairly broad area where the water is about 30 feet deep. If possible, locate this area near a drop off to water nearly twice that deep, or to the maximum depth of the lake. Now find about 40 feet of $\frac{1}{4}$ inch steel cable, or heavy wire. Rope can be used if nothing else is available. Find a dried wooden pole about eight feet long and about four inches in diameter. It should be straight and have the bark peeled off. Use cedar if available.

Bore a hole in the butt end and fasten the cable to it through the hole. Find a rock or other weight that weighs about 50 pounds and is shaped so the wire can be fastened to it very securely. Fasten the wire to the weight. Now load the weight into a good safe boat, but leave the pole and wire out of the boat to float along behind as you row out to your bait station. Two people should go along in the boat if possible. When you get to the preselected place, slide the weight out of the back of the boat. The weight will fall to the bottom of the lake and the pole will act as a easily found buoy. This will mark a permanent location for baiting, which is the next step.

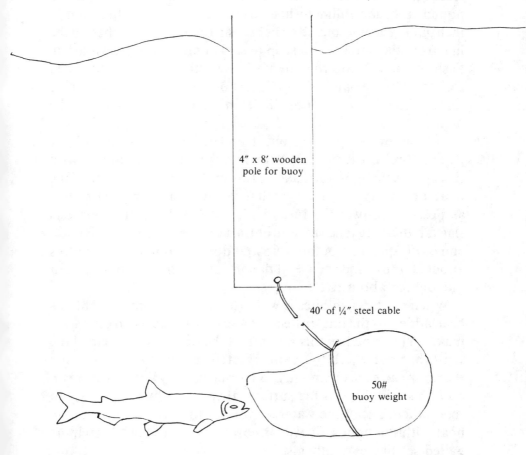

4″ x 8′ wooden
pole for buoy

40′ of ¼″ steel cable

50#
buoy weight

Figure 42.   The all time best method of catching trout and whitefish is to use the buoy system explained here.

Everyday for the next three or four days, go out to the buoy and scatter about one cup of bait around it. Use chopped sucker or smelt meat, tapioca, canned sweet corn, macaroni or even rice. If you use dried corn, soak it overnight before dropping it so it will be soft. Do this for three or four days before you start fishing. This will give cruising schools of fish time to find it and start feeding on the bait. Once they find the abundance of food they will stay nearby or else visit the area at least once a day.

When you start fishing, paddle out to the buoy and tie your boat to it. Don't use a motor to approach the area and don't drop anchor. Either could chase the fish away or make them quit feeding. The tackle should be a spinning outfit with eight to ten pound test monofiliment line. Use a small hook with about ½ inch gape. Put a ½ ounce or lighter sinker about 18 inches up the line from the hook. Use a strip of sucker meat or other white fish flesh for bait. Drop the line until the sinker hits bottom. Then reel up until the bait will dangle just off the bottom. When using this method, leave the line still. Set this line out of the front of the boat.

Take another spinning outfit and tie a Swedish Pimple or jigging lure to the line. Bait the hooks with sweet corn or with fish eggs (spawn) if you have it. Lower this out of the rear of the boat, or wherever you can get that will be as far from the first line as possible. Lower the lure to the bottom. When the line gets slack, indicating it has hit bottom, set the reel so no more line will come off and then pump it up and down about a foot. Do this about 20 times and then let it dangle just off the bottom without moving for about five minutes.

When a whitefish bites it will often feel like some weight has been added to the line, instead of a savage strike like trout might make. When you feel this weight, set the hook with a snap of the wrist, but don't jerk too hard. Whitefish have soft mouths and the hook can easily tear out. Slowly but steadily keep pressure on him and raise him to the surface. Have a landing net handy to scoop them out of the water. If you try to raise the fish into the boat with the hooks, he will almost certainly fall off. Watch the baited set line carefully also.

As the water warms up, probably about the 1st of July, the fish will move to the deepest part of the lake. That is the time to move your buoy also. First, find the deepest water. Then go out to buoy and pull in enough of the anchor wire so the weight is free of the bottom. No need to pull it all the way up. Add a length of wire or cable to reach the bottom at the new depth. Row to the new bait station towing the weight until the new location is reached. Then release it and let it settle into place.

Start over again baiting the new location. In summer small minnows and insects can be used for fishing. If you can catch a female whitefish with eggs, take a small bunch of eggs and a piece of the liver and put them carefully on the hook. Lower it slowly to the bottom, be very careful so the eggs and liver don't come off. I also know that deer, moose and beaver liver meat works good for whitefish bait. As long as the weather stays warm the whitefish will stay around the buoy. If you overfeed the bait station so the baits sour before it is eaten, the fish will abandon the location. Then you must move your buoy and start over again. Lake trout, rainbow trout and suckers also will come to this bait and can be caught.

Lake trout are found in many deep water lakes in the north, and they are fine eating and are easily caught if you can get down to the depths where they live. In winter they will probably be

Figure 43.   The author with a pair of lake trout.

found in about 50 to 60 feet of water. We fish them with small minnows or with jigging lures after cutting a hole in the ice and lowering the bait until it hits bottom. Then we raise it about a foot and jig it up and down.

In spring, lakers often come into shallow water because the water temperature is within their preferable range. They live in water that has a temperature between 48 and 52 degrees, and they will die if they cannot find water under 65 degrees. For this reason lake trout are found only in northern lakes. As summer approaches, the lakers will go as deep as necessary to find water cool enough. In the northern states this is at least 70 to 100 feet.

When the lakers are in the shallows in the spring, they are about as active as they ever get, and they will often bite artificial baits such as spoons and minnow imitations. This is paralleled by the fall spawning period when they also come into shallows and will bite readily. They spawn in water five to fifteen feet deep, starting their spawning activities when the water cools to that temperature. In northern Wisconsin this takes place in November.

In late spring and summer they can be caught by trolling with spinners and cut bait such as a piece of sucker. Either wire line or large sinkers are used to keep the bait down to their depths. In the Great Lakes, downriggers and heavy weights called cannon balls are used to hold the lure to the preferred depth. They also can be caught by fishing right on the bottom with a dead minnow, smelt or other small fish. Lake trout get a considerable amount of their food by picking up dead fish.

King, silver and pink salmon are available to many people now that they are found in the Great Lakes. Most people settling in the northern Great Lakes states will have access to as much salmon and large trout fishing as they want. In the spring just after ice out, the brown trout become active along the shoreline, and can be caught by shore casters and small boat fishermen. Also, at about this time the coho salmon get active along the north shore of Lake Michigan, and in the south shore of Lake Superior. They also can be caught by small boat and shoreline fishermen.

Near the first of May the steelhead will be coming into the

Figure 44.

streams to start their spawning runs. Lake Michigan and Lake Superior have good steelhead runs in many streams. Usually steelheads can't be caught in enough amounts to make them an important food fish, but it is possible to turn them into as few meals.

In May the fishing will really break loose in the Great Lakes, and the entire shore of Lake Superior in Wisconsin, the northshore in Minnesota and southshore in upper Michigan come alive with husky coho, rainbows and brown trout.

Alaska and Canada deep woods residents often have so many fishing opporunities that they can lay in a years supply of fish to smoke or can in a few weeks. However, there are large areas in all states and provinces where the fishing opportunities are poor even though lakes are nearby. Most fishermen don't need to be reminded to find out what fish are available before they decided on place to settle.

Chapter 9.

Free Food From The Woods

Although most woods and wild fields aren't a horn of plenty, where all kinds of wild foods are just laying around ready to be picked up and eaten, as some literature would have you believe, there is definately enough wild plants and fruits available in many areas to be an important supplement to your food supply. It is also possible to live entirely from wild plants for indefinate periods, especially during the harvest season.

In early spring, after the snow melts, some plants will quickly send up green leaves. Watch closely for them and pick the leaves when they are very small, and you can obtain some of the best tasting and vitamin filled salads on the planet.

Wild mustard, white clover, lambs quarter, sour sorrel, dandelions are some plants that speedily present leaves for the picking. This is also the time of the year when it is easily possible to confuse one plant with another, and you could ingest a poisonous or noxious plant, so be sure to know exactly what you are eating before you use the plant.

However, if you are careful there is little danger. I have eaten wild plants in many different states and provinces without even an upset stomach.

The wild mustard family, or winter cress family has about ten species, and all of them are edible. Use the tender green leaves as soon as they show up in the spring by adding a few to a wild salad to give it some tang. The winter cress often can be picked before the snow is gone if it is growing on a bare southern slope.

Mustard leaves left to grow until they are 2 to 3 inches high make good boiling greens also. They have to be boiled quite awhile to make them tender, and of course, you lose some vitamins when they are cooked this way. The flower heads before the blossoms open are also good food. They are picked and washed and boiled for about three minutes. Then they are sprinkled with pepper and salt and seasoned with margarine and eaten.

The dandelion is an easily recognized plant that yields excellent salad material when it first comes up in the spring. It grows under the ground even before the sun shines upon it, obviously responding to the lengthing days. As soon as the snow is gone and sometimes even before the ground is well thawed out, it starts to send up its leaves. At first it looks like a tangle of pinkish red strings, but a few days of sunshine will develop the leaves so they can be identified. If you are going to use them for a salad, pick as soon as they start to develop. Cut the base of the leaves low enough to include the tender white growth of the plant and mix this crisp mellow flavored part with the leaves to tone down their sharp flavor.

As soon as the leaves get 2 inches long, but before the plant blossoms, the leaves make good boiling greens. Pick a good double handful of the young leaves. Be careful to only pick the green leaves, discarding any brown or discolored leaves. Even so, wash and pick them over. Then put them in water that is already boiling and boil for no more then 5 minutes.

Dandelion roots also can be eaten. Dig the roots, wash and peel them and boil until tender. They taste like parsnips, and are usually served with margarine.

Another easily recognized and welcome addition to the wild

food supply is lambs quarter or pigweed. Not to be confused
with burdock, which it slightly resembled, the lambs quarter is a
tall plant with large opposite edible leaves. For that matter, most
of the plant is edible and does not require parboiling. Just pick
the leaves, clean them and cook until they are limp. Lambs
quarter is also a good addition to salads. Only the mature leaves
and stems are tough or bitter. All through the season the tender
tips of the leaves are edible.

Burdock, like pigweed, grows in open areas, sometimes in an
abandoned farm yard. It grows very large and coarse with large
rhubarb-like leaves. When mature, this plant produces a crop of
round bristly seed pods that stick on your clothing when you
walk through them. The young leaves are used as a pot herb. The
roots can be dug and peeled and boiled for a root vegetable. In
fact, it is widely used by orientals, even being cultivated for
culinary puprposes in Japan.

Figure 45.   Burdock leaves.

The miners lettuce was so named because it was used by early miners to ward off scurvy which occurs when the diet does not contain enough vitamin C. It is a low growing plant that in some areas in the north is the most abundant spring edible. This plant is easily recognized because the stem looks like it grows right through the center of the leaves.

When young, this plant can be used like lettuce. When it gets older and tougher it can be boiled for a pot herb.

The common milkweed is a well distributed plant that grows over most of the green regions of the United States and Canada. It might be an unlikely candidate for food to anyone who has tasted the bitter white sap that gives the plant its name. But this sap can be eliminated from the plant by parboiling the parts in a certain way and then the milkweed will yield both asparagus-like vegetable, and broccoli, and a pot herb.

Figure 46.   Milkweed plant showing three edible stages. From left to right; buds, blossoms and pods.

The young plants, early in the spring, make asparagus, the unopened flower buds make a fine substitute for broccoli, and the hard green pods make a good vegetable as a side dish for meat.

First however, the plant parts are picked and washed to remove insects and foreign material. Then a pot of water is placed on the stove and brought to a boil. It is then poured over the plant parts in another pan on the stove. The water is kept boiling for one minute, that water is dumped off, the pot is filled again with boiling water, held to a boil for one minute and then this is dumped. Repeat this once more. Then drain the milkweed plant parts very well and boil them for 10 minutes or until they are tender. The cooked plant parts can be frozen and stored for winter, and if necessary the milkweed could yield a winter supply of vegetables to the cabin dweller.

Another well distributed plant that has graced the table of many backwoodsmen is the fiddle head fern. Ferns are eaten when they are very young before the fronds uncoil to become fern leaves. In fact, after the ferns mature they are poisonous. When they are young enough to resemble a cane or shepards staff, they yield an extremely good tasting vegetable.

Fiddlehead ferns also are very good cooked. They are slightly mucilaginous and can be used to thicken soup or make an okra-like good vegetable. They taste best when they are steamed instead of being boiled. Do this by picking, cleaning, washing and defuzzing a good handful of fiddleheads. Place them in the top of a double boiler containing just enough water to create steam. Place the enclosed container over a pot of boiling water and steam for about 30 minutes. Serve hot with butter if available.

Many wild plants in the north yield a good beverage. The sweet fern makes good tea when steeped in boiling water. Many mint plant, such as peppermint and spearmint leaves are steeped for tea. Wintergreen leaves are steeped in the

Figure 47. Fiddlehead ferns.

sun for tea, sumac drupes can be steeped in cold water, strained and served to make lemonade, and Labador tea grows wild all over the north.

Another well known plant is fireweed, the tall plant with a single sturdy stem and green tapered leaves that resemble willow leaves. The most distinctive part is the beautiful pink or purple flowers that grow at the top of the stem. It grows very rapidly, sometimes covering hundreds of acres where fires have burned the other vegetation. I have walked through acres of it on either side of the Alaska Highway in the Yukon Territory, where forest fires burned the trees and shrubs.

The leaves and stems are edible after they are cooked. The young leaves are cooked into greens and the mature leaves are steeped for tea. The stalk of the plant is peeled and eaten raw or peeled, cut into pieces and cooked in soup.

Early in the spring the cattail sends up the tiny stalks that will eventually ripen into the cattail plant. But, at this emerging stage it is called cossack asparagus, and it can be pulled up and eaten. The edible part is the white stalk. Your taste buds will tell you at what point on the stalk you discard the plant you are eating and pull another. Many cattail marshes have literally tons of this delicious asparagus that goes to waste each year. After the plant gets about 2 feet tall, the stem is too tough to eat completely, but it still contains a tender core that can be peeled out and eaten, either raw or cooked.

In June (in Wisconsin) the cattail will send up one of the best and most abundant food stuffs produced by wild plants, the bloom spike. The bloom spike will go through three stages. Af first the top of the spike will thicken into a tube that will be covered with a husk like an ear of corn. Later the husk will split and the buds will flower into a golden cylinder. When the flowers die, the bloom spike will develop into a hard green tube and finally ripen into the thick brown cattail.

When you notice the cattails developing the tube at the top of the bloom spike, just at the stage when some are starting to split, put on a pair of boots and wade out into the cattail marsh and snap off a pailful of these tiny ears.

They look like tiny ears of corn, and the husks peel away

Figure 48.   Scarlet sumach berries can be used to make a leomade drink.

like the husks from corn, and the cob underneath is covered with blossoms that look like kernals of corn. Drop these peeled cobs into lightly salted, boiling water and boil them for about 10 minutes. Then remove them and eat hot with melted butter, just like an ear of corn. The cob of this ear will be about the size of a piece of wire. These kernals can be cut from the cob and cooked also, as for scalloped corn.

At any season of the year, and this includes the winter, the roots and new shoots of the cattail plant will provide food. Cattail roots are very abundant under most cattail marshes. They look like brown ropes, and in old marshes they almost form a net. At intervals along the brown root will be the new shoots of the cattails. The new shoots are pure white and tapered like a huge animal's tooth. Harvest both of these products by going out into the marsh and digging up the roots with a shovel or burlap bag and harvest a bushel or so. As you pull up the roots, you will uproot some stalks also. These can be cut off but retain the bulb at the bottom of the plant since it also is food.

Now take the roots to water, wash them off very well, snap off the white new shoots if you haven't already and place them in a clean container. Cut the roots into sections about 1 foot long and then peel away the rough, brown, outer skin to expose the starchy core of the root. Now the roots can be baked in an oven until they are dry and brittle. At this stage grind them in a food grinder to the consistency of wheat flour, sift out the fibers and they are a reasonable substitute for wheat flour. The white new shoots can be eaten raw, mixed in salads, cooked as a side dish vegetable, or any other way that you can think of to enjoy their fresh clean taste.

After the cattail blossoms flower, they produce prodigious amounts of pollen. This pollen is an edible product also. Gather it by taking a paper bag going out into a cattail marsh on a windless day (pollen is blown away easily), bend the flowering tubes into the bag and shake them lightly. The pollen will fall into the bag. Keep this up until you have a quart or so. Take the pollen home and run it through a sieve to remove the foreign matter. Then it can be mixed with flour and baked into biscuits, sprinkled over breakfast food or mixed with honey to make cattail candy. It reportedly contains large amounts of vitamin A, but maybe the best part is that it imparts a subtle fresh "corn" taste to whatever it is mixed with.

The cattail is certainly a useful plant to the wild food forager, and it seems unlikely that anyone could starve if they were located close to a good sized cattail marsh.

Another wild plant that will yield an abundance of good food is the acorn. Countless tons of this nutritious food stuff falls to the ground each year, and in many areas only a tiny fraction is utilized by wildlife. The rest could be used by humans without affecting the well being of the wildlife at all.

Acorns grow on all of the 28 species of oaks, but all could be divided into two classes, the trees that bear a crop of acorns every year and those that do it every two or three years. Oaks that bear a crop every year are the sweetest, and where available are best used for human food. However, all acorns are edible after the tannin is leached out. Tannin is the substance that makes acorns bitter, and fortunately it is soluble in water.

The northern cabin dweller could have access to white, Oregon white or burr oak from the white oak group. These oaks have large sweet acorns that mature in one year, or he might have red oak, black oak or pin oak from the red oak family. These acorns mature in two years and are smaller and more bitter.

It is expedient to learn to identify them by studying the local varieties. It only takes one or two good trees to produce all the acorns you want to use. Then when you go out in early autumn to harvest a peck or two you will get the sweetest varities. White oak acorns usually only have to be boiled once to make them sweet. Red oak acorns might have to be boiled three times. However, the following procedure will tame any acorn.

Take the acorns home and remove the shell with a nut cracker and nut pick. Discard the shells and grind the shelled acorns in with a food grinder into coarse meal. Now place about a pint of acorn meal in a large pot, cover with water and bring to a boil. When the water turns very dark brown, dump that water, add more and bring to a boil again. Do this at least three times or until the water doesn't discolor badly when it has boiled for five minutes. Dump the water off, let the meal cool and taste it. If the bitterness is gone, the meal is ready to use. If not, return it to the water and boil it again.

Be sure to record the amounts of water and the length of time you boiled the acorn meal and you can develop an almost fool proof formula for treating the variety of acorns in your area. The finer the acorns are ground, the faster the tannin will leach out, but fine meal is somewhat harder to dry for storage after the boiling.

Cool water also will remove the tannin from acorns. Soak meal for about 48 hours in a cloth bag suspended in an un-polluted, moving water source, such as a brook or spring and have sweet acorn meal without much expediture of your resources. Whole acorns also can be made sweet by soaking them for a week or more. The Indians reportedly buried the acorns in swampy ground and left them all winter to leach. Next spring the tannin was gone and the acorns could be used.

After the acorns are treated, they can be roasted like peanuts, ground fine and used for flour, or used as nut meats in bread and cookies and candies. Probably our favorite recipe is acorn bread. Combine 1 cup of brown sugar, 1 egg, 1 cup of buttermilk, ½ teaspoon of baking soda and 1 teaspoon baking powder, 1 tablespoon melted shortening, ½ teaspoon salt, ¾ cup acorn flour and 1¼ cups white flour. Mix the ingredients together and combine 1 cup coarsely ground, toasted acorn meats. Pour into loaf pan and bake at 350 degrees for one hour.

The time honored tea for reviving winter tired human digestive systems is hemlock tea. Not to be confused with the brew that caused Socrates' demise. North American hemlock tea is brewed from the twigs of the tall northern hemlock, an evergreen that is prized for lumber. The tea from eastern hemlock, western hemlock and mountain hemlock tastes exactly the same to me, and it probably contains comparable amounts of vitamin C. Nobody who drinks a cup of hemlock tea regularly should ever suffer from the lack of vitamin C.

Yellow birch and sweet birch have inner bark and twigs that have a wintergreen flavor and can be used to make wintergreen tea. Just cut a good handful of the tender ends of the twigs, place them in a container and pour boiling water over them. Let steep for 15 minutes, strain out the impurities and enjoy as you would any tea. Where available, the inner bark of both species also can be made into tea or even eaten raw to obtain the considerable amounts of vitamins contained in the inner bark.

Three of the birches have sap that is sweet enough to be made into syrup. This includes yellow birch, sweet birch and paper birch. The sugar content is about ½ as much as the sap from sugar maple trees, but in most areas the availability of dense stands of trees and the considerable amount of sap each tree produces, makes up for the diminished sugar content. They are tapped just like maple trees, and the sap is boiled down until it is sweet enough to satisfy the palate. For the scientific minded, the specific gravity of correctly boiled sap is 31.5. The temperature will be 219 degrees at sea level.

Sugar maple trees are found in Wisconsin, Michigan, Vermont and Maine as well as their surrounding states, and this tree is famous for producing maple syrup and sugar since pre-European days in the United States. For the cabin dweller perhaps operating with a minimum of equipment, this tree offers an opportunity to make not only a years supply of syrup and sugar but the possibility of developing a cash income from the sale of the syrup and sugar. All the equipment required can be purchased for less than $100.00.

Although sugar maple trees have the highest sugar content in their sap, red maple, silver maple, striped maple, mountain maple and big leaf maple also have sweet sap that will yield syrup when boiled down. Big leaf maple grows northward to southeast Alaska. The rest are found south from the Canadian border, and from the east coast west to Minnesota. This information is included to remind the cabin dweller that he probably has trees growing around his cabin in wooded country that will yield sap for making syrup.

One of my favorite native fruits are produced by a formidable shrup called the Hawthorn by botantists. Also known as thorn apple, scarlet haws, thorn plums and several other names, this shrub has at least 100 different species and grows from coast to coast and north to southeastern Alaska.

The fruits resemble tiny apples, and they are a member of the apple family. They ripen after the first frosts and produce copious clusters of delicious tasting small apples. Most produce red or scarlet fruit, but the black Hawthorn that grows north to Alaska has black shiny fruit. They are eaten fresh, made into apple jelly or apple butter, even apple pie. They are somewhat dry, and each fruit contains one or more seeds.

Apple trees that have grown up from discarded or bird scattered apple seeds are apt to be found anywhere in the green regions of the United States. Abandoned farms are often good locations for finding apple trees. Even if the apple trees you find has fruit that doesn't taste good fresh, chances are the fruits will be good when cooked. Very few apples are inedible when cooked.

There are also native North American apples, perhaps the most important in the northwestern regions being the Oregon crab apple that grows into southeastern Alaska.

Here in Wisconsin, we eagerly look forward to fall because the wild plums will be ripening. The species found in the upper midwest and eastern United States is the American and Canadian plum. It is a low growing tree that forms very dense thickets in many locations wherever the soil is rich and moist.

The fruit is red to red purple, very sweet but tart and it makes about the best plum jam that can be found. It is also a fine fruit for eating fresh or for canning up for winter. Pick them when they turn bright red or yellow, after frost in many cases.

Wild strawberries grow over the midwest and northeastern United States and in some part of Canada, and they are about the first berry to ripen, usually being ready to pick by mid-June. Wild strawberries are usually small, but their flavor exceeds any tame strawberry that I have ever eaten. They grow most abundantly in natural or man-made openings where the sun can reach their low growing leaves. Many times the berries are so well hidden by the leaves that you can't see them unless you part the vegetation. Usually if you find a thick patch of strawberry vines, they will bear fruit in season and repeat year after year. Wild strawberries are a bit difficult to pick in large amounts, and we use them for a once-a-year treat. However, we pick from a patch along a pipeline right-of-way and the patch is several miles long and has enough berries to feed a crowd if we had the time and patience to pick them.

A very abundant and easily picked and good tasting fruit grows on the shrub commonly called Juneberries or serviceberries or even Saskatoonberry. Juneberries look like huge blueberries and taste somewhat the same, but they are sweeter and have less juice. The shrubs usually grow on well drained ridges, often in sandy soil, and they might be the dominant woody plant on several acres of land. The shrubs spread from the roots and form a dense clump that might be as big as a pickup truck.

In good bearing years each shrub will produce pecks of fruit, and a stand might have 150 shrubs. It requires no great effort to pick our 30 pint supply that we need for the winter. Juneberries are nearly the only berry that can be picked while standing up. We tie a coffee can around our neck with cloth tape and place the berries in the can as we pick them. This leaves both hands free to snatch the berries.

A somewhat faster way to harvest tree fruits like this is to spread a canvas under the tree and shake the ripe fruit so it falls to the ground. Then pick the canvas up by the ends, trapping the fruit inside. Of course, twigs, leaves and inedible fruit has to be picked out afterward when you do this.

After the Juneberries decline, the raspberries will be ripening, and after they are declining, blueberries mature into delicious blue fruit that attracts bears, birds and every nearby Homo sapien that knows how good they taste. We put up about 10 quarts of blueberries per person, and we thought we were pretty good pickers until we ran into a lady that picked 300 quarts one year by herself. She found a ready market for her surplus too. After the blueberries wind down, the blackberries will be coming on, and it is a great relief after crawling on our hands and knees to pick blueberries and strawberries to be able to stand up and pick the lip smacking, super sweet blackberries. If you can find a patch of large ones, it is possible to pick the years supply in one afternoon.

If possible, put about 100 pints of berries per person, especially if other fruit is hard to come by. Berries can be canned or frozen to preserve them. Blackberries, Juneberries and raspberries are better tasting when they are frozen. Blueberries are more natural tasting when they are canned. Either berry is very easy to preserve, and neither canning or freezing will require any special consideration. Raspberries are decidedly better when they are eaten fresh. In the far north, raspberries often cover large areas after a logging operation or fire has lowered the surrounding vegetation.

In fact, when you decide where you are going to settle, it is expedient to find out if there has been any fires or logging operations nearby in the last four years. These temporary clearings are the natural habitat for raspberries, blueberries and blackberries, as well as the many edible green plants.

Wild cherry trees grow in northern areas of the Lower 48 states and in Canada. Probably the trees that produce the most wild cherries is the black and choke cherry, especially where the trees are growing in an opening so sun can reach the branches.

We know of black cherry trees that will yield a years supply of juice and fruit. The fruits of the black cherry are about ½ inch in diameter. They are very sweet and juicy and yield prodigious amounts of juice that can be made into fruit juice for drinking or flavoring other foods.

Black cherries ripen in September in our area of northern Wisconsin, and probably slightly later further north. If you are watching the tree, the cherries will turn from green to red to black, and some will be found lying on the ground under the tree. This is the time to pick them, and we use a quick method for doing that. We spread canvas under the tree and then use a long pole to whack the branches so the ripe fruit is dislodged and falls to the ground. Usually one tree will yield a three gallon bucket of cherries which is about all we need. They have to be picked over, of course, after they are dropped.

You can separate the cherries from their juice by placing them in a large pan on the stove. Cover with just enough water so they start to float. Then heat the cherries until they split open and release their juice. This is far below the boiling point. Don't boil the fruit, as it will spoil the taste and vitamin content of the juice. When they are hot, place the contents of the pan in a large cheesecloth jelly bag, suspend it over a large container and let the juice drip out for about eight hours. The seeds and pulp that are left should be thrown away. Black cherry seeds contain cyanide-like substance and should not be eaten. Choke cherries are processed the same way.

Most cabineers are surprised at the quantity of wild foods grown around their cabin.

Chapter 10.

Preserving Food

Long before recorded history, man has known how to store food to bridge the gap between the harvest season and the long winter months when food might be scarce. It is not surprising that several different methods have been developed to preserve both vegetable and plant food.

Plant foods are canned, dried, salted and kept at cool temperatures until they are ready to be cooked. Potatoes, rutabagas, parsnips, cabbage, squash, pumpkin and other root crops can be kept for months if held at 35 degrees to 50 degrees, which is about the temperature of the earth below the frost line. The ancients noted this and built underground storage bins which are often called root cellars. In permafrost areas, an underground freezer can be built.

A root cellar is just a hole dug back into a hillside or steep bank, deep enough so the earth will insulate the produce put into it. It can be as big or as small as necessary to store whatever will be placed in it. A root cellar 6' x 8' with 6 foot high ceiling can store all the produce a family of four will need to keep over winter. When you build a root cellar, make sure the drainage is very good so moisture doesn't collect in it. If you can build it in sandy soil, the porous nature of the soil will help speed up drainage problems you might have. Sand is also easier to dig in then hard soil.

The following directions will help you build a 6' x 8' cellar. There should be no reason you can't change the diminsions to suit your own needs also, without causing structural problems.

Digging the hole looks like a formidable task, and it is. If you can arrange to have the dirt removed by machinery, by all means do so. However, one man, reasonably good physical condition, can dig it by hand also if they work more or less regularly for a week. This job will point out the advantages of owning a rubber tired wheelbarrow to wheel the dirt away that you dig out. When the dirt is removed, don't take it too far away because it has to be put back on the top after you start building the frame.

The cabin dweller will probably be building his root cellar from logs, although if lumber is available, there is nothing wrong with using it provided it is treated to resist moisture. If cedar logs are at hand, by all means use them. They will resist decay for 30 years without being treated. However, if cedar isn't available, use the longest lived logs you can find. Cut and peel and get the logs to the excavation. You will need six 10 foot logs for the sides, four 10 foot logs for the ends, two 10 foot logs for the plate, and enough 8 foot logs to cover the top. This will require about sixteen 6 inch logs.

When you have the logs peeled, treat them with used engine oil heated to the steaming point, or use commercial sealer. Treat the logs by painting the liquid on the dried surfaces of the logs with a mop, which can be made of rags. The ends of the poles that will be sunk in the earth can be soaked in oil or copper sulphate liquid by first digging an oversized post hole about 2 feet deep. Line the hole with a heavy duty plastic bag and pour it about half full of oil or copper sulphate solution. Place the pole, butt end down in the hole, (be careful not to puncture the bag) and let it soak to absorb the oil for a week if possible. Make the copper sulphate solution by dissolving 1 pound of crystals of copper sulphate to 3 gallons of water.

These crystals are sold in farm supply stores.

After the logs are treated, you can start building the frame. First, lay out a straight line on the floor of your excavation for one wall of the root cellar, and dig holes 2 feet deep to receive the butts of the side logs. Space the logs about 4 feet apart. It will take three to create an 8 foot sidewall. Measure from this row of upright posts to lay out the other side wall, dig the holes and put the logs in place. Finally, dig in the poles for the rear of the root cellar. A plate log about 10 feet long is placed horizontally across the tops of the side wall to provide a base for the ceilings logs. The side logs have to be sawed evenly after they are in place to receive the plate logs. Also, the plate logs have to be notched to receive the ends of each of the side logs. Use 6 inch spikes to nail the plate log to the side logs.

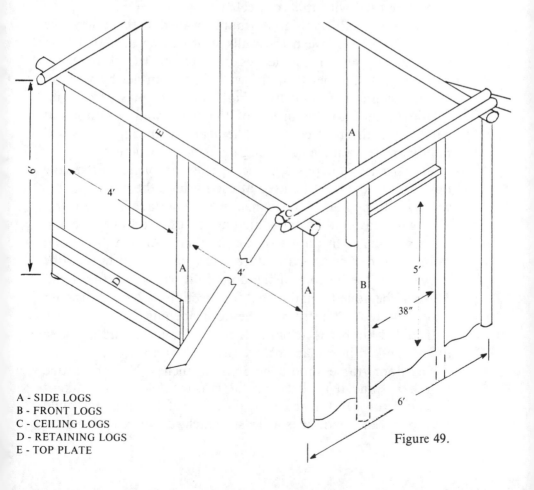

A - SIDE LOGS
B - FRONT LOGS
C - CEILING LOGS
D - RETAINING LOGS
E - TOP PLATE

Figure 49.

With the plate log in place, the next step is to install the ceilings logs, notching the ends of each log as is necessary to provide a firm base on the plate logs. Spike each joint securely as you go. When the ceiling logs are in place, it is time to install whatever retaining walls you need on the side logs to keep the dirt from caving inward. Earth exerts considerable pressure, and at least 2 inch thick lumber is needed to keep loose soil from caving inward. If firm clay soil or extremely rocky soil surrounds the excavation, you might not need a retaining wall.

The front wall will have the door. It will also be exposed to the weather and should be insulated. It will require that the posts for the front wall be set with their inside surfaces about 3 feet apart to provide space for a door. A double door should be used with this root cellar.

The front wall should be double walled with at least 12 inches of space between the walls so it can be insulated. Use sawdust, spagnum moss, leaves, hay, cattail rushes or waste paper to insulate between the walls. You can get by without double walling the front by using 3 inches of plastic foam insulation nailed to the inside of the front wall. Do not put windows in the root cellar, as the heat loss through glass will nullify any advantage of having light in the structure.

The front door poses some special problems. First, the upright logs that will be used at each side of the door opening will have to be hewed or sawn so the flat surface faces inward. This will provide a base for hinging the door on one side and for a weather tight door stop on the other. Also, although no floor is needed in this structure, a door stop will have to be provided at the bottom of the door so it will be weather tight. This will be done by nailing a 3 foot section of 2 x 6 or heavier lumber across the bottom of the door opening.

If milled lumber is at hand, the door frame should be made up and spiked into place before the door is hung.

The door frame should be 36 x 60 inches. Nail the frame together, stand it up between the two front logs and spike it in place. Now carefully measure the inside of the frame and build the door. Make sure it is at least ½ inch narrower and shorter

Figure 50.   Frame for root cellar.

then the frame so the door doesn't bind in the opening.

The door should be constructed of 2 inch lumber or heavy sawmill slabs. If tongue and groove lumber can be used, it will form a tighter more weather proof door. If you can't get tongue and groove lumber, use two layers of boards nailed at right angles to each other with a layer of heavy duty roofing paper nailed between the two layers. Use four heavy strap hinges so it doesn't sag. Foam insulation should be nailed to the inside surface of the door to insulate it.

Some type of venilator will be needed in most climates to keep the shelter from getting excessively damp, especially in summer weather.

We made a venilator from a 30 gallon steel barrel. One end was removed from the barrel and a 2 inch wide, non-continuous slot was chiseled in the sides of the barrel just under the top. These slots were covered with wire screen to keep out insects and small animals. The barrel was centered on the ceiling logs about 3 feet from the rear of the structure. The ceiling logs directly under the barrel were slotted to provide air holes from inside the root cellar to the outside air.

The final steps were to cover the ceiling logs with heavy composition roofing and then shovel the dirt back on the top. It is necessary to put 3 feet of well packed dirt on the top of the cellar. It should be mounded so the water can run away. If sod or grass seed is available, sow a grass cover can be grown on the roof as fast as possible, it will minimize the dirt being blown or washed away.

If you don't care to build a walk-in root cellar, you can produce somewhat the same results by placing your produce in trash barrels or even open ended steel barrels sunk in the ground. Dig in the trash can vertically, 2 feet below the top of the ground on a slope or hillside where water will run off. Put the vegetables or fruit crop that you want to store in the trash can, put the lid on very tightly so moisture can't enter. Shovel 6 inches of dirt over the top of the lid and then pack leaves or straw over top of that to ground level. Also, build up a mound about 2 feet high of leaves and straw, cover the mound with a sheet of heavy duty plastic or canvas and hold down the covering with rocks placed around the edges. When the contents are desired, dig down and get them out.

Once the vegetable bin is opened, it probably won't keep the contents from freezing anymore, so take the entire barrel into the cabin and use up the contents. Be sure to store several foods in each barrel so you have a variety to eat without distrubing the rest.

Potatoes can be grown almost anywhere, and they can provide a substantial part of your diet. It takes about 200 pounds of potatoes for each person for the year. Potatoes and cabbages will keep in trenches dug down into the ground in areas where the ground stays dry. In some places they are just covered

Figure 51. Author with his finished root cellar.

with packed hay or straw to a depth of at least 3 feet. When they are not covered with dirt it is much easier to dig them up.

Purchased or home grown grains, such as wheat and corn or peas and beans are kept in a dry place. They keep very well in the far north, outside in a cache that will exclude mice and red squirrels. A metal garbage can with a tight fitting lid works well for this. They also can be kept in mesh bags inside a rodent proof cache.

Canning is probably the most often used method of preservation by people who live where continuous electric power is not possible. Almost any kind of food can be preserved by heating it to kill any bacteria present in the food, and then keeping it in a sealed container until it is used. Several foods taste better after being canned also. Tough meat, some fruits and vegetables are good examples.

Pint or quart size glass jars are most often used for canning. It will require about 100 quarts jars to can vegetables and fruit to feed one person.

About the most useful object a canning minded cabin dweller can own is a large 9 quart pressure cooker. Meats and fish and poultry should be canned in a pressure cooker because the dread killer botulism can lurk in meat that hasn't been heated to 240 degrees and start growing after many months. A single mouthful of the toxin produced by this germ can kill.

A great wealth of literature already exists on proper canning methods. Try to use only the best unblemished fruits and vegetables for canning, and use unbruised or shot spoiled meat. Many times this is the best way to utilize the toughest cuts of meat, as tough meat will be tenderized and flavored by the canning process.

There are two basic methods of smoking meat. Hot smoking and cold smoking. When the hot smoking method is used, the meat is kept at a high enough temperature to at least partially cook it. Cool smoking is carefully controlling the temperature so the meat does not cook.

Maybe the most economical and durable smoke house can be made from a metal 55 gallon oil barrel. Cut the end from the barrel that has the bungs and cut a hole in the center of the other end, the right size for 6 inch stovepipe or whatever size stovepipe you are going to use. You can cut a steel barrel with a sharp cold chisel and hammer, or have a blacksmith cut it with a burning torch. If the barrel is dirty, burn the inside out first before you use it. Then scrub out the soot and ashes.

Near the top of the barrel, punch holes in the side large enough so wood dowles, sticks or old broom handles can be pushed through from one side to the other to hang large pieces of meat and fish, or to hold a screen for smaller pieces. The rods should be about 4 inches below the top of the barrel. A metal screen can be made from steel mesh or even an old refrigerator or freezer shelf, or if you don't have either you can lay sticks across to hold up rods. You should have about four hold up rods.

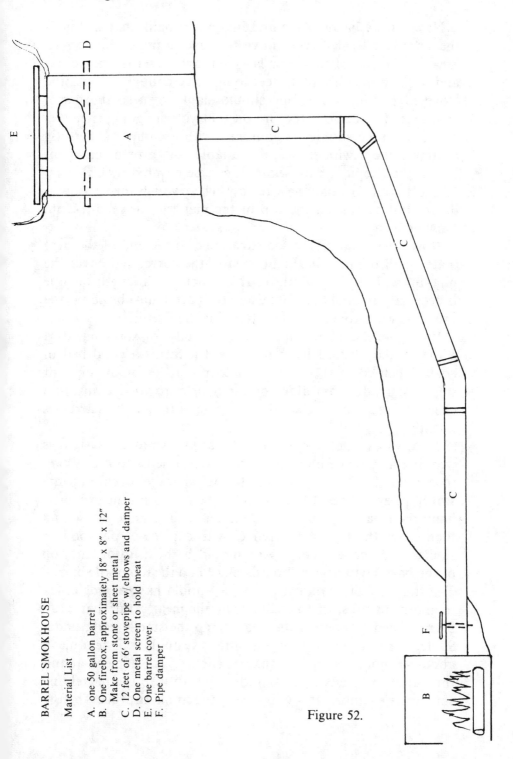

BARREL SMOKHOUSE

Material List

A. one 50 gallon barrel
B. One firebox, approximately 18" x 8" x 12"
   Make from stone or sheet metal
C. 12 feet of 6' stovepipe w/elbows and damper
D. One metal screen to hold meat
E. One barrel cover
F. Pipe damper

Figure 52.

Now set the barrel aside and find a dirt bank that will hold the barrel at least 4 feet above the level ground. Flatten an area on the top of the slope large enough to set the barrel on and dig a trench about 10 feet long, large enough to hold the stove pipe. This stove pipe should slant down so the barrel is at least 4 feet above the fire pit that you are going to make. The stove pipe should be equipped with a damper. Then dig a firepit, line it with stones, if available, and provide an opening so the firepit can draw air. It can be covered with the top of the barrel to hold the fire low when you want to slow it down. Put a rock on the top of the metal lid to keep it from blowing away.

Now set the barrel on the stove pipe so the end of the pipe mates with the hole in the bottom of the barrel and cover the pipe up with dirt by filling in the trench. This length of pipe is necessary to cool the smoke and the barrel must be above the fire so it will provide a good draft for the firepit.

When you have your meat or fish ready for smoking, start a fire in the pit and let it burn until it forms a good bed of coals. Then cover the coals with corn cobs or birch chips, or saw dust made from alder or birch or hardwood chips, and check to see that the smoke is rising through the barrel as intended.

Now watch the smoke to see that the smoking system is working as intended and make any adjustments to the system to correct the flow of smoke. It should travel evenly up the stovepipe and come out the barrel. When it is working properly, hang the meat or place it on a screen in the smoke house and then cover the top of the barrel with a piece of plywood or similar wide cover. This cover should be held up off the top of the barrel with spacer boards placed on the top of the barrel. The first day of smoking, the cover should have a wide crack to allow the moisture to escape from the meat. After that it can be restricted to control the heat. Keep the smoke cool, under 90 degrees most of the time and smoke a shoulder of bear meat, about 48 hours, split fish take 12 hours. Try a piece at this time and if it needs more smoking, return it to the barrel and smoke it somemore. It is well to stop the smoking process before it is overdone since too heavy of a smoking flavor might make it inedible, whereas, if you stop it too soon you can always start it again.

Never use resinous woods for smoking meat. All the pine trees will give off smoke that will render meat nearly inedible. Use alder, apple, maple, birch or most of any of the deciduous woods. Keep green sawdust on hand to cover the fire if possible whenever it starts to burn too high.

The following procedure is used to smoke fish. Clean, wash and wipe dry the fish. Split the large ones into two pieces along the back bone, or fillet them. Prepare a brine by dissolving one cup of noniodized salt in one gallon of water. This will float an egg about ½ inch above the brine. If it sinks lower, add more salt. Prepare one gallon of brine for every four pounds of fish or one quart for each pound. Put the fish in the brine, keep about 40 degrees for 16 hours. Stir the brine occasionally. When you remove the fish from the brine, soak them in fresh cold water for about 30 minutes. This removes the excess salt and blood and hardens the flesh.

After soaking, allow the pieces to drain for about an hour and then place them, skin side down, on the smoking screens. Start the fire, but keep it low until the pellicle forms on the skin. This can be recognized by the shiny coating formed on the flesh.

Fish pieces should be dried in the smoker at 90 degrees to 95 degrees for about an hour. During this time if they are moved, they will not stick to the screen. After two to four hours of smoking, the fish should turn brown and have a substantial pellicle formed. Next, the temperature should be raised to about 225 degrees. This will raise the internal temperature of the flesh to about 190 degrees after three or four hours.

This smoking should continue for at least 12 hours. After this time cool one of the thickest pieces and examine it and taste test to see if it is done. If not, continue to smoke for another 12 hours. Remember, fish smoked by this method are perishable and should be kept in a cooler or refrigerator.

However, fish jerky made by the following method will keep for months without refrigeration if you use lean fish or remove all the fat prior to processing it. Clean, fillet and slice the boneless fillets into strips ½ to ¾ inches wide. Place the fish strips in a brine solution made by dissolving ½ pound of salt in one gallon of water. Be sure the strips are kept completely covered by the solution during the soaking. Keep the brine in a cool place. Forty degrees is the ideal temperature.

Soak the fish strips for at least 12 hours. Longer will do no harm. Remove the strips from the brine and immerse in a large tub of water or place in a clean stream or river for about one hour. Next, place the strips in the smoke box and let them dry (on the surface) for three to four hours. Move the strips occasionally if they stick to the screens (racks.)

Finally, smoke (and dry) the pieces at about 150 degrees for 12 to 14 hours. They are done when they are almost dry, and at which time they should turn brown from the smoke. Remove from the smoke house just before they get too dry to be good eating. Pack in glass jars or sealed plastic bags to keep moisture and dust away from the flesh.

Most any type of meat can be smoked also. It is first cured with salt. The following procedure is designed for curing bear meat. It will work equally well for curing pork. First, chill the meat, using ambient temperature, ice or cold water to cool it to about 39 degrees. The further above the temperature the meat gets, the faster it will spoil, and if it is far below that temperature, the salt won't penetrate the way it should. Allow plenty of time for curing this way. It will take about one minute for either dry salt curing or brine curing. The days per pound formula is; allow four days for each pound of shoulder or ham. For each 25 pounds of hams and shoulders, mix together two pounds (three cups) of pickling salt, ½ cup of brown or white sugar and ½ ounce salt peter. Use ½ the mixture to rub into all surfaces of the meat. Poke it well into the shank end along the bone, and even slit the meat so the salt can get down to the bone since this is the area where spoilage is most apt to take place.

Make the cut along the bone with an internal cut rather then cutting down from the surface. A long boning or filleting knife will work well for this. Poke the salt along the bone with a wooden stick or other instrument that will push the salt mixture deep into the cut. Rub the salt over the outside of the cut so it creates a layer at least ⅛ inch thick, with a thinner coating on the rest of the mix. Very carefully fit the salt coated meat into a sterilized non-metal container, cover it with a wooden loose fitting lid or cheese cloth, and let it cure for a week. Keep the meat cool, between 40 and 35 degrees, if possible. After a week, remove the meat, wipe it dry of liquid and remaining salt and use the other half of the mixture to coat it again. Then pack it again in a barrel or crock.

When you are ready to smoke this meat, remove it from the crock, scrub off the outside salt and wash it. Then hang for 24 hours in a cool airy place until it is done dripping moisture. Then suspend it in the smokehouse and smoke it for about 50 to 60 hours. This should turn the meat a brown all the way through. Taste test it at this stage, and if it doesn't taste right, return it to the smokehouse. Smaller chunks of meat can be salted and smoked the same way.

Some people like to pickle fish. Make a brine from soft pure water, distilled white vinegar with an aetic acid content of at least 4%, and use a high grade pickling salt.

Use fresh cleaned and washed fish. Soak it in the brine made by adding one cup of salt to one gallon of water for one hour. Drain fish, pack in a sterilized glass jar in a strong brine made by mixing 2½ pounds of salt to one gallon of water for 12 hours. Keep cool, then mix up the following ingredients which will be enough for 10 pounds of fish cut in bite sized pieces.

> 1 ounce allspice
> 1 ounce mustard
> ½ pound onions, sliced
> ½ ounce bay leaves
> 2 quarts of distilled white vinegar
> 2 ½ pints of water
> 1 ounce of white pepper
> 1 ounce hot ground or dried peppers

Rinse the salted fish in clean water. Combine the ingredients listed above in a large pan or kettle. Bring to a boil and add the fish. Simmer for ten minutes or until fish is easily pierced with a fork. Remove the fish from the liquid and place in a single layer in a flat pan and cool quickly. Then pack cold fish in a clean jar, adding a few spices, a bay leaf, freshly sliced onions and a slice of lemon. Strain the vinegar solution, bring to a boil and pour into the jars until the fish are covered. Seal the containers with a jar lid. Store in the refrigerator. Use within six weeks.

Fish keep pretty well dried also, as the Eskimos do it. Split the fish down the center, suspend over rods on a drying rack and let it out in the sun or dry air until they are shriveled and hard. They will keep indefinitley like this if kept dry.

Fruits and vegetables can be dried also by placing them between two layers of cheese cloth and putting them out in the sun and air. Protect from moisture and insects. Apple and other large fruits are sliced thin and dried. Berries are dried whole.

Chapter 11.

Prepare For
Medical Emergencies

Although there is hardly an area in this modern age that isn't connected to medical help by radio, with bush planes and helicopters waiting to evacuate anyone from nearly anywhere, there is never-the-less a definite need for emergency medical help. A storm or radio failure can cut off communications. An airplane might not be able to fly, or a doctor could be on vacation or on another case.

Also, many accidents require quick action by a knowledgeable person to save the patient's life if the patient goes into shock or to ease his pain. Heart attacks and bone fractures can happen at any time. Further, it is important to be able to tell when a person is sick and in need of evacuation.

Of course, knowledge will not help much if no medicine or bandages are available, and so a medical kit should be taken into the bush right along with the tools and groceries. It would be hard to improve upon the **medical kits** prescribed by Dr. William Forgey in his excellent book, *Wilderness Medicine,* and so with his permission I will detail both the prescription and non-prescription kits. Either will be adequate.

163

As part of the preparation for going on the trip, each member probably should have a complete medical and dental exam. Also, if members are over 40 years old they should have their eyes checked, particularly the test for glaucoma. Since physical well being is often the direct result of your diet, you should carefully go over your food intake to make sure you are receiving the required amounts of vitamins and minerals. Each adult should check his food intake against the recommended daily amounts as a base for determining if the diet you are following will supply the nutrients that your body needs. Realize that amounts needed by each person vary somewhat and thus the minimum daily recommended allowance means just that. Usually an active person should strive for increased amounts to be certain your body is adequately fed.

When we first took to the woods, I figured out a diet based on the most abundant foods available. It was extremely economical and utilized wild foods as well as potatoes and tomatoes that can be raised in the garden. It supplied every human body requirements as near as I could calculate from the FDA charts. We followed the diet pretty closely, with occasional splurges of junk and exotic foods. We are never sick, not even a cold, and I think this is proof that the diet is adequate. Each reader can do this also, based on the supply of local food.

I also lived almost exclusively on meat and fish for about a dozen years, avoiding sugar in all forms, but including some fruit and some cheese. I fasted for 24 to 36 hours at intrevals of about three months. I felt fine and was seldom sick. Thus, I have proved to my own satisfaction that the human body can be adequately nourished on a diet that is available to the wilderness dweller at very low cost. However, at present there is a great hue and cry about the cholestrol effects of red meat, and perhaps some people, especially if they live sedentary lives, will develop a high cholestrol count. For that reason I am not recommending such a diet for everyone. All I know is that it worked for me.

Along with good nutrition, the woods dweller should learn to be extra careful in all activities. Most accidents are preventable, and a few minutes spent in deciding the safest way to do a task like raising a log or using a knife will prevent most mishaps. I imagine that cutting wood and building are about the most dangerous tasks the woods dweller will perform. Proceed with such tasks as carefully as possible.

Since **cuts** are probably the most common injury, and might require immediate action to stop the bleeding, each member of the family should understand how to deal with them. Almost all bleeding can be controlled by applying pressure directly to the wound. If you stop the flow of blood, nature will cause a clot to form which will also help to stop the flow. Use a sterile bandage or pad if you have time to get one, if not, use the nearest piece of cloth available, even a piece of ripped shirt. Fold it into a pad and press it right against the wound, tight enough to stop the bleeding. Then hold it for at least five minutes. Don't dab at the wound in an attempt to mop up the blood, and don't keep looking at the wound. If a cloth isn't immediately available, press the bare hand directly on the wound to stop the flow of blood until a cloth can be found.

Although a tourniquet is widely publicized, they are seldom if ever necessary, and might well cause more damage than benefit. The only time a tourniquet is necessary is if the bleedling can't be stopped by applying direct pressure.

After the bleeding is stopped, the wound should be cleaned as well as possible. This can be done by washing it with soap and water. Use boiled water that has been cooled. Alcohol and other antiseptics should not be used, as they burn and devitalize the tissue. The cut might start bleeding again after being cleaned, so be sure to have a sterile pad on hand to press into the wound again until the blood clots. If the recommended medical kit is available, use the providine-iodine prep pad to scrub out the wound.

Small cuts can be treated by just applying a dressing and bandage and letting nature take its course, but large cuts must be pulled together with butterfly bandages or by suturing. Most wounds can be held together with butterfly tape, but be sure, when you apply the butterfly bandage, that you pull the wound evenly. If it is pulled unevenly, it will take longer to heal and the result will be an uneven and ugly scar.

The only time suturing should be attempted by an untrained

person, is if the wound can't be pulled together with butterfly bandages so it will hold, and the patient can't be evacuated to trained medical help. Then use the suturing needle and ethilon sutures to pull the wound together. Be sure to have a supply of suturing packages in your kit. The needle and suture are already threaded. Realize that suturing will only cause temporary pain, which will soon disappear and that it can be treated with the Pergogesic tablets in the kit.

The curved suturing needle is not designed to be handled with the fingers. Instead, it is manipulated with the hemostat. The needle is grasped with the hemostat near the base and the point of the needle is pushed down through one side of the wound across the base and up the other side. Be sure to sew it evenly so the wound will pull together evenly. Pull the thread through until about one inch of the cord protrudes, loop the length of the cord over and tie it to the loose end with two or three knots. Snip the cord off and repeat this procedure about ¼ inch further on. Keep this up until the wound is closed. Only use as many stitches as it takes to close the wound. After the cut heals, the stitches have to be cut and removed.

It will be expedient for at least one member of an isolated family or group to practice stitching on a piece of raw meat to get the feel of it.

The needle marks will probably bleed quite well. A little pressure will cause this bleeding to stop. It is not necessary to even worry about this bleeding until the suturing is done. Be sure to sew only through the skin. Avoid the important structures underneath because they can cause nerve damage. If tendons or nerve damage has occured, irrigate the wound thoroughly and stitch it up. Wait until you get to a surgeon to repair the damage. A delay of a week will do no harm.

Use pain killer medication from the kit. Also, it is expedient to give an antibiotic by mouth. Be sure to clean the wound and apply antibiotic ointment. The wound can be kept dressed and should be kept dry until the wound is healed over.

Broken bones are apt to occur in isolated as in settled areas, and a broken bone can range from hardly noticeable, as in the case of a broken toe, to extremely serious, as in the case of the fracture of the leg, neck or back.

Usually if a bone is broken, the victim can feel it, but in some cases it is impossible to tell without X-rays. When a broken bone is suspected to the extremities, it probably should be splinted immediately. Many doctors recommend splinting the break as it is, without an attempt to set the break. Then evacuate the patient to medical help.

Compression splits are available that can be inflated to hold the limb, and they can be a part of every first aid kit. Without compression split, a split can be made of cloth and sticks or boards or a canoe paddle. In most cases, broken bones are not life threatening and can be treated several days after the accident by a physician if the split is put in place to hold the broken ends of the bone from lacerating the surrounding tissue.

However, some fractures produce pressure that shuts off the blood flow to areas of the body, and in this case the fracture should be reduced as much as possible by manipulating the member so circulation will be resumed. Also, some broken bones will protrude through the flesh and can cause serious bleeding.

In this case, thoroughly cleanse the wound with antiseptic, or if you don't have antiseptic, with clean water and cloths. Dress the wound as if it were a cut and apply a split to keep the patient from moving the damage area. Give an antibiotic and evacuate the patient to medical help as soon as possible.

Fractured ribs are quite ocmmon, and are often a result of a blow to the chest or a fall. However, they can occur from a bad cough or sneeze. Usually the patient is aware of the severe pain in the area of the break. Often no treatment is necessary, except the patient should avoid unnecessary movement, wrapping the chest with a towel or undershirt may make it easier to breath. It is important that the patient breath normally so the fluid doesn't accumulate on the lungs, which could lead to pneumonia. The ribs will require six to eight weeks to completely heal.

Animal bites usually occur from handling wild animals. It is almost unheard of for a wild animal to run out of the woods and attack a person. Therefore, most can be prevented by using great care when live animals must be handled.

Every person should have a tetanue toxoid shot before taking to the woods. The wound should be cleaned as soon as possible with soap and water and with a provine-iodine pad. If the skin is punctured, the victim should be put on an antibiotic such as 250 mgs. of Sumycin to be taken four times a day.

A high risk of infection will occur with animal bites, so the wound should never be stitched, but rather closed with butterfly bandages. If an infection occurs, take the tape off the wound and soak the area in warm water or apply hot compresses for 15 minutes at a time, four times a day to draw the infection to the surface. If an abcess forms without drainage, open the abcess with a sterile scapel to allow the pus to escape. Keep covered with sterile dressing except when you are soaking the wound. If an infection develops, double the antibiotic amount or use an antibiotic that is effective for the infection.

A case of **rabies** is always a possibility with an animal bite. If the animal appears unduly exciteable or belligerent, or initates an unprovoked attack on the person, it could be rabid. In particular avoid being bitten by a skunk, since some authorities believe that nearly every skunk has rabies or is a carrier. Dogs, coyotes, fox, squirrel, wildcats and some bats also have transmitted rabies to people. If rabies is even suspected, the patient should report to a physician within two weeks for treatment.

Persons who expect to be working with live wild animals can get a rabies immunization program. Consult your physician for advice on this procedure.

Gun shot wounds should never occur to the experienced woods dweller, primarily because safety measure can be used that will make it extremely unlikely that he gun will discharge at the wrong time or in the wrong direction.

If a person is shot in the backcountry, the location of the wound will determine how he will be treated. If the wound occurs in the chest or abdomen, about the only chance the victim has is to stop the bleeding as much as possible, treat for shock and evacuate to medical help. Often this will be faster than bringing the doctor to the patient, and in the bush the medical help will not have the necessary facilities for treating the patient anyway, and will have to evacuate him.

If a roching shot wound occurs, in which air is sucked in and out with the patient's breathing, the hold should be plugged. One good way to do this is by apply a bandage covered with vasoline over the hole and bandaging it in place. If vasoline isn't available, use butter, margarine or lard to cover the patch, or a piece of plastic.

Heart attack is well known and dreaded malady that can affect nearly anyone, at any time. Usually the symptoms are dramatic. The patient stops doing what he is doing and has the appearance of a very sick individual. The skin may be pale and sweaty and the pulse may be rapid. Often there is severe pain in the chest and upper arms. The attack usually occurs during exertion.

Obviously this needs medical attention and the patient should be evacuated as soon as possible. the most important treatment is to have the patient avoid all activity. If you have a full medical kit, try to control the pain with Tylenol #3, one or two tablets every three hours. 25 mg. of Phenergan can be given to prevent nausea and help sedate the victim. Repeat in four hours.

A **choking** can occur when a piece of meat or other food becomes lodged in the throat. This can be very serious and the obstruction must be removed by whatever means necessary. Often the manual thurst techniques will be successful. Stand the victim up, stand behind him, put your arms around him, interlock the hands into a fist and place the fist in the abdomen just below the chest and give a sudden squeeze. This will cause air to rush from the lungs and can pop the obstruction loose.

If you can't stand the victim up, try to perfrom the manual thrust procedure in whatever position the patient resides.

If the obstruction can't be removed and the patient is clearly dying from lack of air, there is a procedure that could possibly save his life. Make a hole through the trachea with a knife, hold the cut open with a hollow tube of some sort so the air can be breathed in. This is very dangerous and should only be attempted as a last resort. However, if you do attempt, make the hole through the trachea at the center of the windpipe. Make this hole through the cricothyroid membrane which is located just below the Adam's apple, between the Adam's apple and the prominent ring below the Adam's apple called the crico membrane. The hole can be made by pushing the point of the sharpest knife you have or a scapel through the skin and membrane into the opening of the windpipe. The hole has to be kept open.

A device called an Emergency Tracheal Catheter is available. This consists of a needle covered with an external 10 gauge catheter. The catheter is pushed into the crico thyroid membrane and the needle withdrawn, leaving the opening in the catheter for an air hole. This catheter is then taped in place. Any large hollow needle can be used in the same way, and a 12 gauge needle can be taken along in the medical kit for just this emergency.

Many people are anxious about **appendicitis** attacks when they are far from help. An appendicitis attack is clearly a medical emergency, and if possible the patient should be taken to a surgeon immediately. The accurate diagonses of this condition is rather difficult even for a knowledgeable physician, and all the cabineer can do is try. If appendicitis is suspected, evacutate immediately. The symptoms are; the patient first feels a slight pain around the belly button. Within hours the pain gets more severe and localizes in the right lower abdomen. If you push gently on the right lower abdomen, the area will be tense and rigid. Severe tenderness will be experienced by the patient to even slight pushing.

What can you do if you don't have hope of evacuating the patient? Move him as little as possible. Give no food. Provide small amounts of water. The patients best hope is that the appendix will form an abcess that will be walled off from the body by the body defense mechanisms.

As the disease advances, the intestines will stop working and the patient will vomit the contents of the stomach. Vomiting will also aggravate the condition and possibly rupture the appendix, but in the bush there is not much that can be done about it. Some physicians feel that the survival rate, even from a ruptured appedix is as high as 80% without help.

Knowing how to correctly **remove a fish hook** from your flesh might save untold hours of pain and suffering. First, a pair of pliers that can be used to cut the barb off the fish hook is an important item to have along in your tackle box. If the fish hook drives into your skin, push the hook the rest of the way through, following the curve of the hook so it comes out again. Then snip off the barb and remove it by pulling it back out again.

If the victim can stand the pain, the hook also can be removed by placing a loop of fish line in the bend of the hook and pulling the barb straight back out. If a medical kit is available, the area can be numbed with an injection of Xylocaine before this procedure. In the case of a fish hook in or near the eye or other vital areas, it is best to leave the hook in place and tape it or have the victim hold it so it doesn't move. Then evacuate to a surgeon as quickly as possible.

Frostbite occurs when skin tissue freezes. Frostbite can be very shallow, as in the case of skin on the face freezing, or it can be as serious as a completely frozen foot.

In all cases, the frozen part should be thawed as quickly as possible to prevent the frost from going any deeper. If a white patch develops on your face, hold your hand over it until it thaws. If fingers freeze, hold them under your arm or in the groin area until they thaw. If larger parts are frozen, such as a whole foot, thaw it in warm water, about 110 degrees. This is an extremely painful procedure, so give the patient whatever medication is available to ease the pain.

In the case of **extremely deep frostbite**, the member should be kept frozen until there is no possibility that it won't refreeze. When tissue freezes, thaws and refreezes, substantial tissue loss is a certainty. It is better to leave a foot or hand frozen for hours or even days then to thaw them out and have them refreeze. Hardy explorers have walked for days on frozen feet before thawing them, knowing that when they did thaw them out they would be unable to walk.

Thaw deeply frozen limbs in warm water also, warming them up as rapidly as possible. Pain medication can be Tylenol #3, two tablets at the start of the procedure.

A shell or covering that will be black in color will form in the case of severe frostbite. This black covering will gradually fall off with amazingly good healing underneath. Dr. Forgey recommends leaving this black carapace in place. Attempts to remove it surgically will often result in infection, a slower rate of healing and loss of tissue. The frozen digit will gradually amputate itself over a three month period. Complete healing might take six months to a year. Treat for shock, which could occur when the frostbite patient is taken into a warm environment.

Frozen lung occasionally occurs during heavy exertion in extremely cold weather. The lungs are not actually frozen, but the syncronization of the lungs and circulatory system has been upset by chilling. The victim may cough, spit blood and have pain in the shoulders and upper stomach that can last for a week or more.

The treatment is bed rest and steam inhalations, providing humid air to breathe if available. Avoid smoking and exertion.

Hypothermia is the result of lowering the body temperature by getting wet in cold weather or not dressing warmly enough in cold weather or even by not dressing warm enough in moderate weather. Most hypothermia deaths have occured when the temperature was between 30 and 50 degrees.

Proper insulation is the best defense against cold, and most experts recommend wool as being the most efficent insulator even when wet, far surpassing cotton, down or synthetic fibers. Proper rest and nutrition are also factors.

A victim succumbing to hypothermia will start to shiver intensely. He will probably not be able to perform complex tasks such as rewinding a snowshoe lashing. In the next stage, they will continue to shiver even more violently and will have difficulty speaking and thinking. If the condition has persisted until the victim's temperature drops to 90 degrees or below, the shivering will cease and muscle regidity will occur. The exposed skin may turn blue. They will have a complete loss of memory and might loose coordination of the muscles. As the inside body temperature drops lower, the victim will become irrational and finally become unconscious. Death will soon follow.

People have been saved from hypothermia by getting them out of their wet clothing, putting them in a sleeping bag with another person for warmth, or putting them, clothes and all, into a warm bath or running warm water from a shower on them, or by simply bringing them into proximity with a campfire, warm tent or warm room. At any rate, they must be warmed as soon and as rapidly as possible.

A **severe burn** from a campfire or brush fire is a real possibility also. The first reaction should be to immerse the burned area into cold water or snow. Leave it immersed for several minutes. This simple treatment alone can greatly reduce the injury from the burn, and in the case of non-serve burns, it might be the only treatment needed.

Wash the wound with soap and water to clean off all foreign matter. Then lance any blisters and apply a sterile guaze dressing made with 1% Dibucaine ointment to stop the pain. This dressing should be changed every 48 hours.

A severely burned patient may go into shock if not treated and this is serious enough to take precedence over wound treatment. Shock prevention can best be accomplished by replacing the lost fluids. The best way to do this is in the wilderness is by having the patient drink all the water he can. Sip almost continuously, if possible. The amount needed will be about five quarts in the first eight hours and another five quarts over the next 16 hours. Keep the patient as comfortable as possible, and evacuate immediately.

If possible at least one member of a family should learn the techniques of first aid and how to administer the medicine contained in the kit. Then the learned can teach the other members of the family.

Chances are great that you will never have a medical emergency, but having the knowledge and medicine to handle the emergency can keep it from becoming a tragedy if it does occur.

A **tooth ache** can occur from a lost filling, a cavity or as a result of a blow to the mouth. Immediate relief usually can be obtained by cleaning the cavity or tooth and applying oil of cloves directly to the affected part. A good pain remedy such as Tylenol #3 also will deaden the pain. When a filling is lost, it can be replaced by installing a temporary filling. The temporary filling is made by mixing zinc oxide powder and oil of gloves. Pack this material into the cavity and allow it to harden for 24 hours without disturbing it by biting on that side of the mouth.

An antibiotic such as Sumycin (250 mgs) one tablet, four times daily should be given where infection could be present.

Medical Kits

BASIC KIT — Prescription

RX before an item indicates that a prescription must be obtain for its purchase.

RX	Cortisporin ophthalmic ⅛th ounce tube	1 to 3 tubes
RX	Phenergan tablets, 25 mg	10 to 30 tablets
	Bisacodyl tablets, 5 mg	10 tablets
RX	Pontocaine ophthalmic .5% ointment, ⅛th ounce tube	1 tube
	Camalox tablets	20 to 40 tablets
RX	Sumycin tablets, 250 mg - or E.E.S. 400 tablets	40 to 100 tablets
RX	Tylenol #3 tablets	10 to 30 tablets
	Actifed tablets	40 tablets
	Povidone-iodine Prep Pads	10 pads
	Bandages 1″ x 3″ (plastic strips)	20 each
	Guaze pads, 12 ply, 3″ x 3″, sterile	20 each
	Guaze roll, 3″ x 10 yards, sterile	1 each
	Elastic Bandages, 4″ x 10 yards, top quality	1 each
	Butterfly bandages, medium	10 each
	Moleskin, 2″ x 12″ strip	1 each
	Tape, 1″ x 10 yards	1 roll

AUGMENTATION KIT

RX	Anakit, Hollister-Stier Co.	1 kit
	Triple Antibiotic Ointment, 1½ gram packs	10 each

Hibiclens Surgical Scrub	2 to 4 ounces
Cutter Snake Bite Kit	1 kit
Vaseline Gauze, 3" x 9", sterile	3 each
Needle Holder, Mayo-Hegar	1 each
Bandage Scissors, Lister, or Operating Scissors	1 only
Scalpel, Disposable, #10 or #11, sterile	1 only
Splinter Forceps	1 each
Ethilon Suture, 3-0	3 packs
Ethilon Suture, 5-0	3 packs
Plain Gut Suture, 3-0	1 pack
Tinactin Ointment 1%, 15 gram tube	1 tube
RX Xylocaine for injection, 2% plain, 30 ml bottle	1 bottle
RX Syringe, 3½ ml size with 25 gauge needle	2 each

BASIC KIT - Nonprescription

Percogesic	24 to 48 tablests
Pseudoephedrine 30 mg	50 tablets
Chlorpheniramine 4 mg	25 tablets
Yellow Oxide of Mercury ophthalmic 1%, ⅛th oz tube	1 tube
Schein Otic Drops (or equal), 1 ounce bottle	1 bottle
Triple Antibiotic Ointment, 1½ ounce packets	10 packets
Dibucaine Ointment 1%, 15 gram tube	1 tube
Meclizine 25 mg tablets	10 tablets
Bacid Capsules	20 to 30 capsules
Bisacodyl tablets, 5 mg	10 tablets
Camalox tablets	20 to 40 tablets
Povidone-oidine Prep Pads	10 pads
Bandages, 1" x 3" (plastic strips)	20 each
Gauze pads, 12 ply, 3" x 3", sterile	20 each
Gauze rolls, 3" x 10 yards, sterile	1 each
Elastic Bandage, 4" x 10 yards, top quality	1 each
Butterfly bandages, medium	10 each
Moleskin, 2" x 12" strip	1 each
Tape, 1" x 10 yards	1 roll

AUGMENTATION KIT

Vaseline Gauze, sterile 3″ x 9″	3 each
Hibiclens Surgical Scrub	½ to 4 ounces
Needle Holder, Mayo-Hegar	1 each
Bandage Scissors, Lister-or Operating Scissors	1 only
Scalpel, disposable, #10 or #11, sterile	1 only
Splinter Forceps	1 each
Ethilon Suture, 3-0	3 packs
Ethilon Suture, 5-0	3 packs
Plain Gut Suture, 3-0	1 pack
Cutter Snake Bite Kit	1 kit
Tinactin Ointment 1%, 15 gram tube	1 tube
Tooth Ache Gel, ⅛th ounce	1 tube

INDEX